Where We Live Now

Where We Live Now

*Immigration and Race
in the United States*

John Iceland

UNIVERSITY OF CALIFORNIA PRESS

Berkeley   Los Angeles   London

University of California Press, one of the most
distinguished university presses in the United States,
enriches lives around the world by advancing scholar-
ship in the humanities, social sciences, and natural
sciences. Its activities are supported by the UC Press
Foundation and by philanthropic contributions from
individuals and institutions. For more information,
visit www.ucpress.edu.

University of California Press
Berkeley and Los Angeles, California

University of California Press, Ltd.
London, England

Library of Congress Cataloging-in-Publication Data

Iceland, John, 1970–.
    Where we live now : immigration and race in the United
States / John Iceland.
        p.   cm.
    Includes bibliographical references and index.
    ISBN 978-0-520-25762-7 (cloth : alk. paper)
    ISBN 978-0-520-25763-4 (pbk. : alk. paper)
        1. Immigrants—Housing—United States.
2. Discrimination in housing—United States.   3. Ethnic
neighborhoods—United States.   4. Assimilation
(Sociology)—United States.   5. Hispanic Americans—
Cultural assimilation.   I. Title.

HD7288.72.U5134   2009

304.8'73—dc22   2008035899

Manufactured in the United States of America

17   16   15   14   13   12   11   10   09
10   9   8   7   6   5   4   3   2   1

The paper used in this publication meets the minimum
requirements of ANSI/NISO z39.48–1992 (R 1997)
(Permanence of Paper).

For Jeannie, Jakob, and Mia

CONTENTS

FIGURES

TABLES

ACKNOWLEDGMENTS

I would like to begin by expressing the intellectual debt I owe to researchers who inspired my original interest in these issues—Reynolds Farley, Michael White, Douglas Massey, and Nancy Denton, who by turns wrote so beautifully, clearly, and powerfully about residential segregation in America's metropolitan areas.

There are a number of others who have played important roles in the production of the work here. Daniel Weinberg at the U.S. Census Bureau provided me with the opportunity to work with him on a Census Bureau monograph concerning residential segregation after the 2000 census. That work laid the foundation for all of my subsequent research on segregation issues. Rima Wilkes and I coauthored papers on hypersegregation and the role of socioeconomic status in shaping residential patterns. Jeffrey Timberlake led a joint effort that looked at trends in racial and ethnic residential inequality. Erika Steinmetz not only did a tremendous amount of work on the census monograph but also provided vital support for follow-up working papers and publications. Melissa Scopilliti and Kyle Anne Nelson have proved to be valuable collaborators and coauthors on papers that directly informed the analyses in this book.

I would like to give special thanks to Naomi Schneider at the University of California Press, who provided crucial support for this project during the publication process.

Most of all, I would like to thank my friends and family for their support and encouragement, including my wife, Jean, who motivated me to write this book. I would also like to thank my children, Jakob and Mia, who, with my wife, helped keep me grounded by reminding me of what's really important. I also owe so much gratitude to my parents, Harry and Joan, and the rest of my family: Charles, Debbie, Matthew, Josh, and of course Matt, John, and Edna.

Funding for this project came from NIH grant Ro1 HD 0489047-01, as well as from a subcontract with Sabre Systems Inc., which used funds provided by the Census Bureau.

CHAPTER I

Introduction

Racial and ethnic diversity is a fact of life in a growing number of American cities and communities. A short twenty-minute ride (depending on the traffic!) along Fort Hamilton Parkway in Brooklyn, New York—where some of my family lives—illustrates this. Along some portions of the trip one can catch sight of a significant number of Chinese-owned stores; in others one sees Orthodox Jews going about their business in traditional black attire; and in yet others different ethnic groups appear to work and reside. For example, in one of the neighborhoods that abuts the parkway, 47 percent of the residents are foreign-born. Of that 47 percent, 40 percent are from Europe, 36 percent from Asia, 20 percent from Latin America, and the rest from other countries, mainly Canada and Australia.[1]

New York City has been a traditional immigrant destination. Recently, however, neighborhoods in other cities have emerged as immigrant destinations as well. In the Mt. Pleasant neighborhood of Washington, D.C., Salvadoran immigrants live adjacent to African Americans and whites, with sections of the neighborhood occupied by all groups. Silver Spring, Maryland—just outside of the Washington, D.C., limits, where I resided until recently—is also a mixing bowl: close to 40 percent of the population is non-Hispanic white, with blacks, Asians, and Hispanics well represented among the rest.[2]

Although immigrants remain relatively concentrated in certain areas, such as Los Angeles, Washington, D.C., and New York City, racial and ethnic concentrations declined in the 1990s and 2000s, and diversity has increased in most parts of the United States.[3] For instance, states such as Georgia and North Carolina, which certainly do not have reputations as immigrant destinations, were in the top ten among states with the highest net increase in immigrant residents between 2000 and 2003, with each receiving more than 100,000 in that period.[4]

To a cosmopolitan person, the increasing diversity of many American metropolitan areas may be a source of stimulation. It can afford the opportunity to eat a variety of foods, observe different customs, and share in others' celebrations, such as Cinco de Mayo or Chinese New Year. With these opportunities, however, also comes the potential for conflict. Groups often compete for scarce local resources, such as municipal jobs or funds for community organizations and activities. Cultural and political differences can lead to clashing viewpoints.

A Newark, New Jersey, newspaper ran an article in 2006 on the vast demographic changes in northern New Jersey. "At the start of this decade," wrote the *Star Ledger,* "northern New Jersey was one of the most diverse, yet one of the most segregated, regions of the country, according to demographic studies. As it becomes even more diverse, sociologists and others are watching to see if it becomes more integrated residentially—or whether segregation persists."[5] The article goes on to tell the stories of several residents. For example, after a divorce Maria Guareno, a physical therapist from Colombia, moved to Wharton, New Jersey (where her cousin already lived) with two children. The article quotes her daughter, Paola, a senior at Morris Hills High School, who says she likes school but often feels socially isolated: "I don't fit in with the white kids because I'm Spanish, but I don't fit in with a lot of the Spanish kids because I speak English." The Guarenos add that although they haven't faced any overt discrimination, they sometimes sense the distrustful stares of store merchants and non-Latino neighbors.

Roger Smith, an African American, moved his family from Newark to Union Township in 2002. Smith is a youth worker for a nonprofit agency in Essex County. "The education I got growing up wasn't the best," he told the paper. "That's why we moved to Union. . . . I wanted a multiracial community. . . . In Union, everybody is getting along with each other. Neighbors talk to each other. You won't find neighborhoods dominated by one ethnic group anymore. Them days are winding down." His daughter, who is in second grade, has Indian, Brazilian, African, and African American classmates. Smith added, "It's an amazing sight to see, and the best part is, you see them all getting along with each other."

One of the central goals of this book is to examine whether neighborhood-level segregation persists and what role immigration is playing in changing residential patterns in the United States. In general, it is unsurprising that different racial, ethnic, and immigrant groups often display distinct residential patterns. Some forms of segregation may be quite benign, because people of similar backgrounds often prefer to live near each other. Nevertheless, high levels of segregation, particularly if resulting from discrimination, can exacerbate racial and ethnic inequality. Historically, high levels of black-white segregation served to limit the residential choices of African Americans as well as constrain their economic and educational opportunities. This situation led many people to support the Supreme Court's 1954 *Brown v. Board of Education* finding, which invalidated "separate but equal" treatment.

A number of studies have shown that during the past few decades there have been moderate declines in black-white residential segregation in U.S. metropolitan areas.[6] However, this has been accompanied by small increases in the segregation of Asians and Hispanics from whites. What explains these patterns? On the one hand, we might expect that in the post-1960s civil rights era, racial and ethnic polarization would decline for all groups. On the other hand, some have argued that continued high levels of immigration bolster Hispanic and Asian ethnic enclaves, in part because of the immigration process itself and also as a result of socioeconomic differences between the foreign-born newcomers and the native-born white population.

This book delves into these issues by examining how immigration has reshaped the metropolitan landscape and how the interplay between the racial, ethnic, and class composition of both the native and immigrant populations further molds residential patterns. Much of the analysis is based on my own examination of data from multiple decennial censuses and other household surveys. I also review and incorporate findings from other studies on these issues. The Washington, D.C., metropolitan area is at times invoked as a case study, as it embodies recent ongoing social processes, such as population growth via immigration and momentous changes in racial, ethnic, and class diversity.

In short, the questions tackled in the following chapters are: Is there evidence that immigrants are becoming residentially assimilated? Does the incorporation process look different for immigrants of different racial and ethnic backgrounds? How do other characteristics of immigrants, such as English-language ability and socioeconomic standing, affect the extent of residential segregation? What has been the impact of immigration on the segregation patterns of native-born blacks and whites? How stable are diverse neighborhoods, and what is the quality of group relations in diverse areas?

In this book I show that immigrant groups and their descendants are by and large becoming residentially assimilated in American metropolitan areas. For example, native-born Hispanics, Asians, and blacks are all less segregated from whites than are the foreign-born of these groups. Immigrants who have been in the United States for a longer period of time are also generally less segregated from other groups than new arrivals. Socioeconomic differences play an important role in explaining these patterns and trends for all racial and ethnic groups—especially for Hispanics and Asians. Those of higher socioeconomic status are substantially less segregated from whites than lower-socioeconomic-status individuals. Over time we may see greater integration if members of these groups move up the socioeconomic ladder in the coming years.

A second finding is that in many cases we see *multiple* forms of assimilation and incorporation. For example, some analyses in this book indicate that native-born Hispanics are less segregated from both Anglos *and* African Americans than foreign-born Hispanics. Moreover, Hispanic race groups also show particularly low levels of segregation from native-born Hispanics not of their own race, indicating the salience of pan-Hispanic identity across country of origin and also self-identified race groups. In diverse societies, it is important to recognize that different immigrant groups can become integrated with multiple other groups.

A third finding is that extent and pace of spatial assimilation among immigrants are nevertheless still substantially shaped by race and ethnicity. For example, levels of segregation from native-born non-Hispanic whites are highest among black immigrants and lowest among white immigrants. Hispanic and Asian immigrants fall in between. Moreover, "assimilation" does not always suggest the same process for all groups. For example, among racially diverse Hispanic immigrants, those who identify themselves as "white" or "other" race are considerably less segregated from non-Hispanic whites than those who report being "black." Conversely, for black Hispanic immigrants, assimilation may mean slight declines in segregation from whites over time and across generations, but even larger declines in segregation from non-Hispanic blacks. In fact, the very high overall levels of segregation between Anglos and black Hispanics and black immigrants more generally to a large extent overshadow the slight generational convergence. Some of the findings herein are thus as consistent with the *segmented assimilation* perspective (described in more detail in chapter 2) as with spatial assimilation. In other words, immigrant groups to some extent experience divergent patterns of incorporation in the United States depending on their race and ethnicity.

These findings have implications for racial stratification in the United States. They suggest that we may see racial and ethnic boundary "blurring" or "shifting" among some groups in the coming years. Boundary blurring refers to a process by which the social boundary between groups becomes less distinct over time. This occurs when there is frequent contact, such as daily interactions and, ultimately, intermarriage between groups. If such contact occurs on a large enough scale, boundaries can shift, where a population once on one side of a boundary moves to the other.[7] This is precisely what occurred among many immigrant groups from southern and eastern Europe in the early twentieth century. At the time of their entry, such immigrants were considered racially distinct from the native-born white population (which was largely from northern and western Europe) but over time became accepted as whites.[8] In this book, I provide evidence of boundary blurring, especially between some non-black Hispanics and non-Hispanic whites. Segregation between whites and Asians is also moderate, and patterns observed are generally consistent with residential assimilation.

Interestingly, the growing diversity in metropolitan America, fueled by immigration, has had important implications for the most rigid of color lines—that between whites and blacks. In the last major book on residential segregation, *American Apartheid* (1993), Douglas Massey and Nancy Denton effectively argued how the problem of the twentieth century was indeed, as foreseen by W. E. B. Du Bois at the dawn of the century, that of the color line.[9] Massey and Denton documented how the extremely high levels of residential segregation between whites and blacks (which they termed "hypersegregation") were reinforced by racism and discrimination in the real-estate industry, banking institutions, and the everyday acts of individuals. One of the themes in my book, however, is that—in concert with broader political, economic, and cultural shifts—immigration has softened the black-white divide. In particular, black segregation from other groups, including whites, tends to be lower in multiethnic metropolitan areas. Although the reasons for this are not entirely clear, some researchers have hypothesized that Hispanics and Asians may serve as "buffers" between whites and blacks.[10] The presence of multiple minority groups may moderate the stark black-white divide that dominated in the past, thereby helping reduce—if even moderately—the tension in black-white relations. Multiethnic metropolitan areas are also often newer urban areas in the South and West, which experience fewer historically entrenched black-white divisions.

Because of immigration, whites are also considerably less likely than in the past to live in all-white neighborhoods in many metropolitan areas. While the sharing of residential space can lead to conflict over local governance and use of community resources, such exposure has also led to multiracial coalitions built on shared interests. For example, groups often share the goal of living in safe neighborhoods, with satisfactory housing and good public education, and work together toward these ends.[11]

Despite these trends, I remain cautious about drawing firm conclusions concerning the effects of immigration on black-white segregation and the inevitability of spatial assimilation of immigrants in American neighborhoods. First, despite some declines in black segregation in recent decades, blacks and black immigrants continue to be more segregated from whites than other groups. Black-white racial polarization and the continued—albeit declining—discrimination against blacks in the housing market still play important roles in shaping residential patterns.[12] Whether the long-run trend of moderate declines in black segregation continues and eventually translates into greater integration for black immigrants and their children will be an important issue to track in the coming years.

Second, that acculturation indicators (such as English-language ability) and socioeconomic characteristics often help explain relatively high levels of segregation among some groups—and Hispanic immigrants in particular—also has important implications. On the one hand, these indicators suggest that spatial assimilation processes are at work that could reduce Hispanic-white segregation over the longer run as Hispanics achieve economic upward mobility. On the other hand, high levels of Hispanic immigration, largely consisting of people of lower socioeconomic status—precisely the characteristics associated with high levels of segregation—suggest that we will in fact witness increasing levels of segregation for Hispanics in the short and medium term. If negative economic, political, or social trauma served to either inhibit future Hispanic socioeconomic mobility or heighten tensions between Hispanics and other groups, then diminishing levels of segregation would be far from assured. It is not difficult to envision a future in which Hispanic distinctiveness is reinforced by continued immigration and, over the long term, is reflected in higher levels of residential segregation and social distance from other groups.

WHAT IS RESIDENTIAL SEGREGATION?

Before delving into residential segregation patterns, it is important to define what *residential segregation* means. The term generally refers to the differential distribution of groups across space and is usually thought of in terms of the degree to which various groups reside in different neighborhoods. People are residentially segregated across a number of socioeconomic and demographic characteristics, including age, income, and—the focus here—race, ethnicity, and nativity. It is commonly thought that differences in residential patterns across racial and ethnic groups reflect social distance.[13] Researchers at times look at regional patterns of settlement to gauge to what extent immigrants are spatially assimilating in the United States.[14] While exploring regional patterns can be informative, an analysis of neighborhood-level patterns of settlement—the focus of this book—likely provides a better barometer of various groups' residential assimilation because it measures social distance within housing markets (this issue is discussed in more detail in chapter 2).

The residential patterns of minority groups have been studied for many decades. W. E. B. Du Bois, for example, documented the residential patterns of blacks in Philadelphia's Seventh Ward in his 1899 book, *The Philadelphia Negro*.[15] Louis Wirth's *The Ghetto*, published in 1928, compared the similarities between the Jewish ghettos in Europe with those in Chicago.[16] Karl and Alma Taeuber noted in 1965 that new immigrants to the United States in the nineteenth and early twentieth centuries were by and large poor and poorly educated. They often lived in ethnic enclaves in low-rent areas.[17]

While the term *residential segregation* clearly denotes some level of physical separation, there are actually many ways to measure segregation, and the measures themselves tap into different dimensions of this separation. Throughout this book I rely on a number of complementary measures to provide a nuanced view of how residential patterns have changed over time.

CONSEQUENCES OF SEGREGATION

Studying segregation is important in large part because of the consequences of segregation. A number of studies have documented the strong link between black-white segregation and black disadvantage. Massey and Denton effectively argued that segregation helps perpetuate and reinforce concentrated African American poverty.[18] David Cutler and Edward Glaeser, in a rigorous statistical analysis of these issues, found that black-white segregation is specifically linked to lower high-school graduation rates among blacks, higher joblessness, lower earnings, and greater levels of single parenthood. They also found only a slight positive effect, at most, of segregation on outcomes among whites. For example, whites in cities with high and low levels of black-white segregation fared similarly.[19] Overall, black-white residential segregation has been found to constrain the residential choices available to African Americans, limit their access to good schools and jobs, negatively impact their health and academic performance, and contribute to their social exclusion and alienation.[20]

That many immigrants and their children today are segregated from other groups does not in itself signal an immense social crisis or indicate that immigrants are facing discrimination and disadvantage. New immigrants often settle in ethnic enclaves because these areas provide a familiar environment filled with other people who share a common culture and view of life. Ethnic economic networks also attract newcomers to ethnic enclaves. Immigrants therefore often draw strength from their ethnic communities.

Nevertheless, residential segregation could also cause and reflect divisions across communities. Residential segregation becomes particularly problematic if it concentrates disadvantage and is associated with overlapping inequalities. For example, if spatially concentrated immigrants face multiple problems, such as high rates of joblessness, underrepresentation in government, and social stigmatization, this could reinforce social distance and increase alienation among later generations.

The 2005 immigrant riots in France illustrate how social, economic, and spatial isolation can lead to conflict. Many low-income immigrants in Paris, for example, live in isolated suburban public-housing communities where levels of unemployment are high and hopes for the future are low. The sense of alienation is often stronger among the second and subsequent generations. They may see the economic promise of their adopted country but be unable to attain it. Their national communities provide the sense of belonging that is otherwise lacking in the wider culture, thus reinforcing residential segregation and heightening the potential for conflict.

One need not look as far as Europe to see the potential for conflict. Douglas Massey has argued that Mexican Americans are at risk of becoming a new urban underclass because of their relatively high levels of segregation from other groups, coupled with relatively low levels of educational attainment and wages. About a fifth of Mexican Americans are also undocumented immigrants and thus vulnerable to exploitation and exclusion. These factors, he holds, spell trouble for the long-run incorporation of Mexican Americans in the United States.[21] It is therefore essential to take a closer look at the extent of and recent changes in the segregation experienced by immigrants and their children to discern what patterns of incorporation we may expect in the future.

PLAN OF THE BOOK

Chapter 2 provides a historical overview of immigrant settlement patterns and a review of theories of immigrant residential incorporation. The most prominent perspective that arose in the early part of the twentieth century was *assimilation theory*. Assimilation essentially refers to the reduction in group differences over time and plays out in several dimensions, including in economic, cultural, political, and residential spheres. The last is of course the focus of this book, though at times other dimensions of assimilation are also discussed. In recent decades other theories have challenged the assimilation perspective. Some argue that recent waves of immigrants experience greater *ethnic disadvantage* (or *ethnic retention*) than those of past waves, and that we will likely witness relatively little assimilation between new immigrants and the host population. Others have posited that *segmented assimilation* best explains patterns of immigrant incorporation. While some immigrants, according to this theory, will be readily assimilated with whites along many dimensions in the years after their arrival, others will retain their ethnic distinctiveness, and yet others, due to blocked opportunities, may assimilate downward into what has been a predominately African American underclass.

Chapter 3 begins with a description of the changing racial and ethnic composition of the United States in the post-1965 period, when laws governing immigration were radically changed. I examine general patterns and trends in racial and ethnic residential segregation over the past few decades: how black-white segregation has declined, but Hispanic-white and Asian-white segregation has increased by many measures. I also discuss the importance of socioeconomic differences between groups in shaping residential patterns.

Chapter 4 carefully looks at the association between immigration and segregation. I find that among blacks, Hispanics, and Asians, the foreign-born tend to be more segregated from whites than the native-born, providing support for assimilation theory. For all groups, resources also matter: those with greater income are more likely than lower-income immigrants to share neighborhoods with whites. However, there are significant differences in the *extent* of segregation from whites, with black immigrants in particular displaying very high levels of segregation.

In chapter 5 I take a closer look at how race shapes residential patterns among Hispanics. For example, are black Hispanics very different from white Hispanics in their segregation from non-Hispanic whites (at times termed *Anglos* for the sake of simplicity)? I also examine multiple forms of assimilation: to what extent various Hispanic subgroups share neighborhoods not only with Anglos but also with blacks and other Hispanics. I describe how Hispanic race groups often experience multiple and concurrent forms of spatial assimilation: native-born white, black, and other-race Hispanics are all less segregated from both Anglos *and* African Americans than are the foreign-born of the respective groups. The one exception is a modest distancing observed between black Hispanics and certain other Hispanic groups across generations. On the whole, the implication of these findings is that assimilation is reducing (though not in all instances) the significance of various color lines in metropolitan America.

Chapter 6 examines a set of related issues concerning the effects of growing diversity on American communities. Whites are less likely to live in homogeneous neighborhoods than they did thirty or forty years ago. For blacks, growing diversity has not only translated into living in neighborhoods with other minorities but also been associated with moderately lower levels of segregation from whites. The coexistence of multiple groups may be helping to reduce the historical black-white divide in American society. However, diversity can also increase segregation—certainly in the short run—between Asians, Hispanics, whites, and other groups when diversity is fueled by growing numbers of new immigrants, who are particularly likely to live in ethnic enclaves.

While many metropolitan neighborhoods continue to display the traditional pattern of "invasion and succession"—whereby the entrance of minority members results in "white flight"—there are a growing number of stable diverse communities. That is not to say that diversity necessarily translates into harmony. Ethnic conflict is common in diverse areas, and conflict is often exacerbated by class differences between groups. Despite this, ethnic groups that share residential space also at times work together because they share common goals associated with neighborhood improvement. Chapter 6 ends with an examination of the residential patterns of mixed-race individuals, who generally live in more diverse neighborhoods than whites or blacks—a pattern consistent with spatial assimilation.

Chapter 7, the conclusion, reviews the main findings and discusses their implications for the trajectory of the color line. Patterns of spatial assimilation described in the previous chapters, along with trends in ethnic intermarriage, suggest that we may observe a blurring of the color line in the coming years. While we may see an emergence of a "black-nonblack" divide—where blacks are uniquely disadvantaged—we may see a more general attenuation of differences across groups. I note a number of reasons to be cautious about this conclusion, such as continued large-scale immigration to the United States that includes a significant number of low-skill workers whose economic prospects—and the fortunes of their families—are uncertain. I end with a discussion of potentially productive avenues for future research on these issues.

CHAPTER 2

Historical Overview and Theories of Immigrant Spatial Incorporation

Immigration has continually reshaped the racial and ethnic character of the United States. The earliest settlers from Europe to America migrated to a fairly sparsely populated land and eventually took from the Native Americans by force what they could not obtain otherwise. From the start of the colonial period in 1607, to the adoption of the Constitution in 1789, close to a million people came to the United States—about 600,000 from Europe and perhaps 300,000 Africans.[1] At the time of the first U.S. census, in 1790, about 60 percent of the population was from England, but many were also from Scotland, Germany, the Netherlands, and France. Voluntary migrants came to the colonies for a variety of religious, economic, and political reasons, such as the anticipation of economic opportunity or freedom from religious persecution.[2]

During the colonial period, migrants from England not only impressed the largest demographic stamp on the area that eventually became the United States but also exerted the greatest cultural, social, and political influence. As Philip Martin and Elizabeth Midgley note: "They [the English colonists] built communities at Jamestown and Plymouth, seized control from the Dutch in New York, and overran various French and Spanish settlements. These colonists established English as the public language and England's common law as the model for the U.S. legal system."[3]

While the English imprint was clearly the most significant in these early years, Americans developed a distinct identity over time. This identity was in large part a function of the mixing of cultures, as was noted by observers.[4] This notion of an *American* identity, then, reflects not simply the assimilation of new immigrants into an English culture but also the emergence of a culture influenced by the population's multiple origins.

At the same time, immigrants and their children retained elements of their previous cultures, if to differing degrees. Even as immigrants became acculturated to their new environment, they still often lived in distinct communities with particular institutions and economic niches. Irish immigrants in the nineteenth century, for example, were concentrated in large cities such as Boston and New York, were overrepresented as common laborers and domestic servants and later on in government occupations (such as the police force), and established numerous Irish Catholic churches.[5] These twin and often competing forces in the residential sphere—assimilation and ethnic retention—are the focus of this chapter.

HISTORICAL SETTLEMENT PATTERNS

Regional Concentrations

It has long been noted that immigrants of different origins are often concentrated in different regions of the United States. For example, in their book, *Immigrant America*, Alejandro Portes and Ruben Rumbaut describe that it is hardly an accident that European immigrants first settled in states along the Atlantic seaboard, while Asian immigrants populated the Pacific Rim states, and Latin American immigrants con-

centrated in the Southwest.[6] Settling in areas with greater proximity to
the country of origin lowered both the cost of moving to the United
States and the cost of the return trip home.

In colonial times there were also distinct regional differences in
settlement patterns among European immigrants. The English were
particularly well represented in New England states, although they
were present in large numbers in all of the colonies. Germans were
concentrated in Pennsylvania, the Dutch in New York and New Jersey,
and the relatively small number of Swedes in Delaware. Black slaves,
who were of course mainly involuntary migrants, were overwhelmingly
concentrated in the South. For example, they constituted over two-
fifths of the populations of South Carolina and Virginia in 1790.[7]

In the nineteenth century the Irish tended to settle in the large cities,
mainly in New England, New York, and New Jersey, though not exclusively. In contrast, German immigrants in the nineteenth century were
considerably less urban and much more concentrated in the Midwest,
in states such as Wisconsin and Ohio. Scandinavian immigrants flocked
to midwestern and north-central states, particularly Minnesota. Polish
immigrants of the late nineteenth and early twentieth centuries settled
in large eastern and midwestern cities such as Chicago, New York,
Pittsburgh, and Buffalo. A vast majority of both Chinese and Japanese
immigrants in the nineteenth century lived along the Pacific coast,
with a strong concentration in California. Mexican immigrants of the
early 1900s not only settled in border states but also moved to cities in
the Midwest such as Chicago, Milwaukee, and Gary, Indiana.[8]

Regional concentrations, then, stemmed not only from proximity
to one's home country but also from established ethnic concentrations
and the economic conditions of the communities they settled in at the
time of entry.[9] Ethnic networks drew people to established communities, where compatriots helped the newcomers find housing and jobs.
The growing industrial power of midwestern cities in the nineteenth
and early twentieth centuries drew immigrants of many origins to
those cities.

Residential Patterns within Metropolitan Areas

Examining *regional* settlement patterns is informative for a couple of reasons. Ethnic identity is more likely to be reinforced by living in a region with many members of one's own ethnic group (known as *coethnics*) than by living in one with few. In addition, when a particular group occupies an area for many generations, that area may become associated with distinct cultural traits.[10] However, there are limitations to drawing conclusions about the spatial assimilation of immigrants based on regional patterns alone. Groups may be overrepresented in different regions but still display relatively little social and cultural difference from each other, especially over time. For example, while Poles remain concentrated in the Northeast and Midwest today, they show low degrees of neighborhood-level segregation from other white ethnic groups in the metropolitan areas where they reside.[11] Conversely, other groups may live in the same metropolitan areas as one another, but may still live worlds apart. Even though blacks and whites are highly represented in many of the same metropolitan areas, neighborhood-level black-white segregation is on average quite prevalent, which is indicative of the level of racism, and quality of black-white relations more generally, in the United States.[12]

Sociologists grew increasingly interested in the social organization and functioning of communities within metropolitan areas in the early decades of the twentieth century. The neighborhood was seen as shaping the opportunities and constraints individuals faced in their everyday life and was the basis for both political participation and control.[13] In 1925, Robert Park wrote about how neighborhood residential segregation and racial and ethnic divisions more generally reinforced immigrant group solidarity:

> The isolation of the immigrant and racial colonies of the so-called ghettos and areas of population segregation tend to preserve and, where there is racial prejudice, to intensify the intimacies and solidarity of the local and neighborhood groups. Where individuals of

the same race or of the same vocation live together in segregated groups, neighborhood sentiment tends to fuse together with racial antagonisms and class interests. Physical and sentimental distances reinforce each other, and the influences of local distribution of the population participate with the influences of class and race in the evolution of the social organization.[14]

Robert Park, Ernest Burgess, and other sociologists at the University of Chicago were particularly interested in how new migrants to Chicago became incorporated into the city's life. They were largely responsible for developing the *assimilation* paradigm for understanding this incorporation process. They saw assimilation as the "process of interpenetration and fusion in which persons and groups acquire the memories, sentiments, and attitudes of other persons and groups and, by sharing their experience and history, are incorporated into the mainstream of American life."[15]

These sociologists held that immigrants were likely to assimilate into the host society over the long run. In 1964 Milton Gordon provided a systematic discussion of the assimilation concept and identified seven dimensions of assimilation in his widely cited book, *Assimilation in American Life.* In his view there was a critical difference between "acculturation" and "structural assimilation." He referred to acculturation as the minority group's adoption of the cultural patterns of the host society, whereas structural assimilation was the entry of members of an ethnic minority into primary-group relationships, such as close friendships and intermarriage, with the majority group. Gordon discussed at length the importance of prejudice and discrimination in contributing to social distance between groups. Nevertheless, he argued that American-born children of immigrants were by and large "irreversibly" on the path to complete acculturation, though not necessarily structural assimilation.[16] He did, however, note that the barrier between blacks and whites was more formidable, a fact also long-recognized by other commentators.

BLACK SEGREGATION
AND BLACK EXCEPTIONALISM

W. E. B. Du Bois conducted one of the earliest sociological investigations of African American residential patterns, among other topics, in *The Philadelphia Negro*, published in 1899. He reported that, according to the 1890 census, nearly forty thousand blacks lived in Philadelphia, and about a quarter of them lived in the Seventh Ward. Another quarter lived in three adjoining wards. He described the Seventh Ward as a "thickly populated district of varying character," with business and residential sections of the city to the north, middle- and working-class neighborhoods to the south, the wharf and industry to the west, and "Negro, Italian, and Jewish slums" to the east.[17] While this was before the proliferation of far-flung suburbs made possible by a vast system of highways, Philadelphia was clearly, like most cities of the day with substantial black populations, residentially and socially deeply divided by race.

With the decline in immigration after the 1920s, studies on segregation in the post–World War II era tended to focus on the segregation of blacks from whites rather than the immigrant experience. Gunnar Myrdal, in his unflinching *American Dilemma: The Negro Problem and Modern Democracy*, published in 1944, described the extent of prejudice, discrimination, and segregation in the United States. He noted that intermarriage was prohibited by law in all southern states and enforced either by the courts or by lynching. Residential segregation also played an important role in keeping social distance. "Because Negro people do not live near white people," he wrote, "they cannot—even if they otherwise would—associate with each other in the many activities founded on common neighborhood."[18] Thus, segregation resulted in single-race schools, hospitals, and other institutions. He described how discrimination, poverty, and "ethnic attachments" among blacks led to their residential concentration, although he emphasized that discrimination was by far the most important factor: "The Negro individual is not allowed to move out of a 'Negro' neighborhood. The question whether the average Negro 'wants' to live among his own kind then becomes largely an academic one, as we have no means of ascertaining what he would want if he were free to choose. In this sense practically all the statistically observed Negro housing concentration is, in essence, forced segregation, independent of the factors which have brought it out."[19]

Karl and Alma Taeuber's 1965 volume, *Negroes in Cities*, provided another impressive and thorough examination of general patterns of black-white segregation and the role of social and economic factors in producing these patterns. The Taeubers described how the process of residential assimilation did not apply to the large waves of black migrants from the South to northern cities in the early and mid-twentieth century. In fact, during the first few decades of the twentieth century, segregation between blacks and whites in metropolitan areas actually increased, largely due to white suburbanization coupled with continued discrimination.[20] African Americans remained concentrated in low-status positions because they faced a range of social, economic, and residential barriers that were higher than those faced by immigrants. The Taeubers noted that "a high degree of racial residential segregation is universal in American cities. Whether a city is a metropolitan center or a suburb; whether it is in the North or South; whether the Negro population is large or small—in every case, white and Negro households are highly segregated from each other. . . . In fact, Negroes are by far the most residentially segregated urban minority group in recent American history."[21]

In a 1980 study comparing blacks with the late nineteenth- and early twentieth-century wave of European immigrants, Stanley Lieberson found that until around 1910, immigrants were actually at first more isolated from other groups in northern cities than blacks were. He described how the new immigrants initially had strong incentives to self-segregate while they became acculturated to the new society. The black population in many northern cities was also still relatively small at that time, and thus not seen as a threat to the white population. Between 1910 and 1920, however, the isolation of new European immigrants was on the decline, whereas blacks became increasingly isolated, indicating a sharp shift in the positions of these populations.[22]

In their 1993 book, *American Apartheid*, Douglas Massey and Nancy Denton built upon the work of the Taeubers, Lieberson, and Kenneth Clark's 1965 *Dark Ghetto* (which likewise chronicled the segregation of African Americans in the ghetto).[23] Massey and Denton described how racism and discrimination perpetuated extremely high levels of black-white segregation, which they termed "hypersegregation." They forcefully argued that "this extreme isolation [of African Americans] did not just happen; it was manufactured by whites through a series of self-conscious actions and purposeful institutional arrangements that continue today."[24]

Massey and Denton described how, historically, segregation in the South was enforced by whites with the Jim Crow system, a "set of laws and informal expectations that subordinated blacks to whites in all areas of social and economic life."[25] In the North, segregation developed because of white-dominated real-estate practices and because of the violence directed toward blacks who entered formerly white neighborhoods. For example, between 1900 and 1920 there were a series of race riots in a number of cities (New York City in 1900, Springfield, Illinois, in 1908, Chicago in 1919, among others), in which many African Americans living outside of "black" neighborhoods had their houses destroyed.

In some areas, white neighborhood "improvement associations" used a variety of tools to keep African Americans out, such as boycotting real-estate agents who sold homes to blacks. They sometimes also implemented "restrictive covenants," which were contractual agreements among property owners whereby they would not sell or lease their houses to black home seekers. Local real-estate boards also sometimes took the lead in establishing their own restrictive covenants.[26]

Massey and Denton further argued that discrimination against blacks in housing and lending markets, even though illegal in the wake of civil rights legislation, continued to greatly constrict African American housing options: "In the aftermath of the civil rights revolution, few whites voiced openly racist sentiments; realtors no longer refused outright to rent or sell to blacks. . . . This lack of overt racism, however, did not mean that prejudice and discrimination had ended; although racist attitudes and behaviors went underground, they did not disappear."[27] For example, African American home seekers to this day are generally showed fewer properties and are steered toward certain neighborhoods with more African Americans. They may receive inferior service (such as being shown fewer properties) or offered no assistance in arranging financing. Continuing discrimination and segregation, Massey and Denton argued, has severely undermined the social and economic well-being of African Americans.

The black-white view of segregation that dominated the writing on residential issues in the middle decades of the twentieth century has gradually given way to multiethnic perspectives (also exhibited in the work of Massey and Denton). In particular, the rapid growth of the Hispanic and Asian populations since the 1960s, in part in response to changes in immigration policy, has spurred increased interest in the residential patterns of these groups in American society. Indeed, Hispanics surpassed African Americans as the largest minority group in the United States in 2003.[28]

The degree to which recent immigrants to the United States and their children will become assimilated into American society remains contested. Some argue, among other things, that immigrants in the post-1965 period are more racially distinct from the host society than past waves of immigrants and will thus be highly marginalized from whites in a way that may come closer to the experience of African Americans.[29] Others contend that differences between earlier and more recent waves of immigration tend to be overstated, and that assimilation theory continues to provide valuable insights about patterns of incorporation of recent immigrants.[30]

THEORIES OF IMMIGRANT INCORPORATION
AND RESIDENTIAL SEGREGATION

Three common theoretical perspectives are used to explain how immigrants and their children become incorporated into society: assimilation, ethnic disadvantage (or ethnic retention), and segmented assimilation.

Assimilation

Assimilation refers to the decline of ethnic distinctions between groups. Classic assimilation theory posits that ethnic immigrant groups experience integration with a society's majority group through the adoption of mainstream attitudes and culture, and through educational and work experiences. Contemporary assimilation theorists emphasize that assimilation need not be a one-way street, where minority members become more like the majority group members, which in the United States consists of non-Hispanic whites. Rather, assimilation involves a general convergence of social, economic, and cultural patterns.[31]

Spatial assimilation refers to the convergence of residential patterns in particular. Upon their arrival, immigrants may be residentially segregated from other groups for a variety of reasons. Social networks, both kin and community, are key factors shaping where immigrants live.[32] Immigrants often feel more comfortable living with, and welcomed by, their fellow coethnics. In addition, the low socioeconomic status of many immigrants may mean that such individuals may simply not be able to afford to live in the same neighborhoods as more affluent whites. People with little education or few skills—attributes usually referred to as "human capital"—may be particularly dependent on their ethnic communities. In contrast, immigrants who are professionals, such as scientists and engineers, are likely to rely less on ethnic networks and more on the ties they develop with a particular employer.[33]

According to the spatial assimilation model, immigrants are more likely to move out of ethnic communities as they become acculturated with the host society and as they achieve socioeconomic upward mobility. For example, as immigrants become more familiar with local norms and as their English-language ability improves, they may become more comfortable interacting with others and living outside of their ethnic enclave. Immigrants may also become more familiar with the amenities of alternative neighborhoods, such as good schools and clean streets, and, if their own socioeconomic standing allows it, they may be more likely to move to those areas, which often contain members of other ethnic groups. The result is a dispersion of immigrant group members and desegregation over time.[34]

Richard Alba and Victor Nee, in their discussion of assimilation theory, explain how assimilation is not necessarily a universal outcome for all groups. Moreover, assimilation is a lengthy process that typically spans generations: "To the extent that assimilation occurs, it proceeds incrementally as an intergenerational process, stemming both from individuals' purposive action and from the unintended consequences of their workaday decisions. In the case of immigrants and their descendants who may not intentionally seek to assimilate, the cumulative effect of pragmatic decisions aimed at successful adaptation can give rise to changes in behavior that nevertheless lead to eventual assimilation."[35]

Spatial assimilation theory offers clear and testable hypotheses concerning the residential patterns of immigrants. Residential exposure to the majority group is expected to increase the longer immigrants are in the host country and across generations. The quality of neighborhoods of residence is likewise expected to improve with socioeconomic mobility and acculturation.[36]

There is considerable evidence that the descendants of European immigrants of the nineteenth and early twentieth centuries have largely assimilated into U.S. society. While certainly some groups remain concentrated in particular regions of the country, white ethnic groups tend to share many of the same neighborhoods within the metropolitan areas where they reside.[37]

However, just because white immigrants of the previous great wave of immigration have assimilated does not mean that post-1965 immigrants will have the same experience. Commentators have pointed to a number of differences in the conditions under which these assorted waves arrived in the United States. For example, some argue that the hiatus in immigration that began in the 1920s, following the passage of tough immigration restrictions by Congress, served to weaken ethnic communities. Ethnic enclaves no longer received new members who could replace individuals departing to outlying areas. With regard to the more recent wave of immigration, Alba and Nee note that despite the very important exception of Mexico, there has been a shift in immigrants' countries of origin ever since 1965, such as a decrease in the number of immigrants from Korea and Taiwan and increases in the number from other countries, such as El Salvador and Guatemala. Such continual shifts in flows result in a very diverse immigration stream that tends to undermine the formation of large ethnic enclaves.

Another feature of current immigration that some argue works against assimilation is the racial distinctiveness of new immigrant groups. The argument is that while the previous wave of immigrants hailed from many different countries, they were more racially homogeneous. The counterargument is that race is largely a social construct, and a reading of historical accounts indicates that many groups of the previous wave of immigration, including the Irish, Jews, and Italians, were usually perceived as racially distinct from the majority of native-born Americans. As historian Roger Daniels writes: "However curious it may seem today, by the late nineteenth century many of the 'best and brightest' minds in America had become convinced that of all the many 'races' (we would say 'ethnic groups') of Europe one alone—variously called Anglo-Saxon, Aryan, Teutonic, or Nordic—had superior innate characteristics. Often using a crude misapplication of Darwinian evolution, which substituted these various 'races' for Darwinian species, historians, political scientists, economists, and, later, eugenicists discovered that democratic political institutions had developed and could thrive only among Anglo-Saxon peoples."[38]

The notion that immigrants from different European countries constituted different races dissipated only over time as various groups achieved political, social, and economic mobility. In addition, eugenic theories that were in style at the time lost favor in the wake of Hitler's defeat in World War II, Hitler having been a champion of eugenics.[39]

There are other possible differences in the conditions immigrants face that may affect patterns of assimilation today. Some argue that high levels of income inequality will hinder the socioeconomic mobility of recent immigrants and their children. However, levels of income inequality were also high in the 1920s. Others mention differences in the ideological climate regarding ethnic diversity, such as greater support for multiculturalism and less pressure to assimilate in recent decades, which may in turn weaken the assimilation process. Some counter that the ideological climate may actually facilitate the incorporation process. The ideal of tolerating the cultural differences between groups may serve to reduce tensions and the social distance between groups over the longer run.

Still others argue that the emergence of transnationalism, where immigrant communities may span national borders, makes it less likely that immigrants will assimilate in the host country. Yet ties have long existed between immigrants in the host country and their kin and communities in the sending country. Daniels estimates that emigration from the United States to countries of origin varied considerably across groups. For example, between 30 to 50 percent of Italian immigrants returned to Italy, compared with fewer than 5 percent of Jewish immigrants. Greeks also had strong ties to Greece, and perhaps a little over half emigrated back to Greece.[40] Alba and Nee, in an extended discussion of the distinctions between eras of immigration, conclude that, while not unimportant, such differences are not as clear-cut as often thought, and likely do not undermine the predictive power of assimilation theory.[41] Others do not share this view.

Ethnic Disadvantage

Assimilation was the dominant theory of immigrant incorporation until the 1960s and 1970s, when it came under attack for empirical and political reasons. Empirically, some researchers pointed to the persistent subordination of some groups in American society—particularly African Americans. Politically, this was a time of celebration of group differences and rebellion against the politics of conformity. Assimilation theory was taken as a criticism of the unique contributions of minorities and immigrants.[42] Indeed, even the term *assimilation*—which to some implies the repudiation of one's culture and origins—has been out of fashion in the academic literature on immigrant *incorporation* or *integration*.

In contrast to assimilation theory, the ethnic disadvantage (or ethnic retention) model holds that increasing knowledge of the language of the new country and familiarity with its culture and customs often do not lead to increasing assimilation. For one thing, lingering discrimination and structural barriers to opportunities often hamper the assimilation process. Differential access to wealth, power, and privilege affect how well immigrants fare in the host country and may impede their full incorporation into American society.[43]

In research on ethnic residential patterns, the offshoot of the ethnic disadvantage theory is termed *place stratification*. This perspective likewise emphasizes that lingering prejudice and discrimination by the dominant group (non-Hispanic whites in the U.S. context) prevent neighborhood-level integration. Segregation is the tool used by whites to maintain social distance from minority groups. The effects of structural barriers are thought to be greatest for blacks in the United States because blacks have historically been perceived in the most unfavorable terms.[44]

The desire of minority group members to live with their coethnics plays a role in continuing segregation. In studies of individuals' preferences to live in neighborhoods with varying degrees of integration, sociologist Camille Charles describes how respondents of all races tend to express a desire to live near people of the same ethnicity. However, whites tend to exhibit a stronger preference than Hispanics, blacks, and Asians for same-race neighbors and would be less comfortable as a numerical minority. Since each minority group has a preference for a greater number of coethnic neighbors than most whites could tolerate in their own neighborhood, this likely often leads to "tipping" toward a majority-race makeup rather than a stable neighborhood mix. In these studies of racial preferences, whites also tend to be the most desirable out-group (group other than a certain group's own), while blacks are the least desirable, suggesting a racial rank ordering of residential preferences.[45]

Discriminatory practices in the housing market against African Americans in particular, as well as Hispanics and Asians, have been well documented.[46] As described earlier, over the years these discriminatory practices have included real-estate agents steering racial groups to certain neighborhoods, providing less information and assistance to minority home seekers, the provision of unequal access to mortgage credit, and neighbors' hostility.[47] Research has indicated both a willingness of whites to live in more integrated neighborhoods and a decline in discrimination in the housing market in recent years. Changing attitudes in society, the rising economic status of minority customers, and the continuing effect of the Fair Housing Act on the real-estate industry and the law's enforcement all likely play a role in these trends.[48] However, despite some declines in discrimination, many believe that both it and white avoidance of mixed or minority neighborhoods still play a central role in shaping the residential patterns of various ethnic groups in the United States.[49]

Segmented Assimilation

A third theory of immigrant incorporation is segmented assimilation. This perspective focuses on divergent patterns of incorporation among contemporary immigrants. It grew out of studies that found that many of the disadvantages faced by poor immigrant families were sometimes reproduced or even enhanced in the next generation. For example, the prevalence of female heads of household increased across generations among many Latin American nationality groups in the United States. This suggests that acculturation may do little to reduce disadvantage, and in some cases may exacerbate it if the ethnic group members adopt norms of the host society, such as nonmarital childbearing, that do not enhance the well-being of the next generation.[50]

According to the segmented assimilation perspective, the host society offers uneven possibilities to different immigrant groups. Recent immigrants are being absorbed by different segments of American society, ranging from affluent middle-class suburbs to impoverished inner-city ghettos. Individual- and structural-level factors play key roles in affecting the incorporation process, and there is an important interaction between the two levels. Individual-level factors include education, career aspiration, English-language ability, place of birth, age on arrival, and length of residence in the United States. Immigrants who arrive at a young age and whose parents have high levels of education and English-language ability, for example, are more likely to achieve socioeconomic success as adults and to assimilate into "mainstream" society. Children of immigrants with low levels of education who themselves arrived as teenagers are less likely to achieve the same kind of socioeconomic success. In response to a perceived lack of opportunities, immigrants may cultivate ties with their ethnic communities in order to achieve upward mobility rather than try to integrate into the mainstream.[51]

Structural-level factors that likewise affect patterns of incorporation include racial stratification and the range of economic opportunities available in a particular place at a particular time. As discussed earlier, racial discrimination may diminish the opportunities available to non-white immigrants. Increasing income inequality in the United States has also had a negative impact on the earnings of immigrants with low levels of education. Thus, according to the segmented assimilation model, we should expect to see considerable differences in residential patterns for various immigrant groups, with some groups experiencing no decline in their residential segregation from non-Hispanic whites over time, while others will more readily assimilate into the mainstream.

These three theoretical models—assimilation, ethnic disadvantage, and segmented assimilation—provide us with alternative ways of understanding immigrant incorporation in the United States. The following chapters review the evidence regarding which is the most useful for understanding the residential patterns of immigrants. As a result, we will get a better sense of not only what patterns we see today in U.S. metropolitan areas but also what we might expect in the future, in terms of both integration and the possible trajectory of the American color line. If segregation is low and declining among some groups, this would suggest that the social boundaries between groups are becoming less distinct—and less important—over time. However, if we see little evidence of residential integration, the implication is that social boundaries between groups will likewise remain strong in the coming years.

CHAPTER 3

Immigration, Diversity, and Patterns of Racial and Ethnic Residential Segregation

The United States has become markedly more racially diverse over the past few decades. The proportion of the population that is non-Hispanic white declined from 83 percent in 1970 to 76 percent in 1990 and to about 67 percent in 2005. This figure is projected to decline to around 52 percent by 2050.[1] In 2005, 14 percent of the U.S. population was Hispanic, another 13 percent African American, 5 percent Asian, and about 1 percent American Indian. The trend toward increasing diversity is even more visible in some of the nation's largest cities, many of which are now "majority minority"—where the number of minority residents now surpasses the number of non-Hispanic whites. For example, in one-third of the nation's largest metropolitan areas at least half of all children belonged to racial and ethnic minorities in 2004. These include metropolitan areas such as Washington, D.C., Las Vegas, and Tucson, which until relatively recently had not been immigrant magnets.[2] Indeed, immigration from Asia and Latin America has played a large role in this growing diversity. The rapid increase of the Asian population, and the more recent rise in the black immigrant population, is a result of immigration reform in 1965, which ended a system of national quotas that favored immigration from Europe.

In this chapter, I describe how the history of U.S. immigration policy has affected patterns of neighborhood-level residential segregation, and how race and ethnicity continue to play important roles in shaping residential patterns. However, the socioeconomic characteristics of different groups help determine, to a moderate degree, the extent of their segregation from whites, a pattern that is increasingly true for African Americans. Over the last three decades of the twentieth century we generally witnessed a decline in black exceptionalism in residential patterns, though blacks continue to be more disadvantaged than Asians and Hispanics. Asians and Hispanics saw little decline in their segregation from whites in the same period—and increases by many measures—raising questions about the role that immigration is playing in shaping these residential patterns.

IMMIGRATION POLICY

The United States had a laissez-faire policy toward immigration from its founding until 1875. The Naturalization Act of 1790 allowed immigrants to acquire citizenship after several years of residence, and there were no legal restrictions on the number of immigrants or on places of origin. However, in the middle decades of the nineteenth century there were growing pockets of anti-immigrant sentiment, particularly with the rise in the number of Roman Catholic immigrants from Ireland and Germany. Anti-Catholic sentiment occasionally turned violent, such as in the destruction of Catholic churches in the 1850s in places such as Sidney, Ohio, and Dorchester, Massachusetts. Politically, the anti-immigration forces coalesced into the American (or "Know Nothing") Party of the 1840s and early 1850s, which called for the stiffening of naturalization laws. These efforts were generally unsuccessful.[3]

By the late nineteenth century there was widespread unease with the number of immigrants streaming into the United States from southern and eastern Europe, and on the West Coast there was considerable opposition to immigration from Asia. The first qualitative restriction against immigration was the barring of convicts and prostitutes in 1875. This was followed by the more far-ranging Immigration Act of 1882, which prohibited immigration from China. This act, rooted in racial prejudice, was passed in response to complaints from workers in California who opposed "unfair competition" from Chinese immigrants.[4]

In 1897 Congress passed a bill imposing a literacy test on immigrants in an effort to prevent the more "undesirable" immigrants, mainly from eastern and southern Europe, from entering the country. The bill was vetoed by President Grover Cleveland, a principled and generally underappreciated American president. As Cleveland biographer Alyn Brodsky writes: "Signing the bill would have earned Cleveland more plaudits than any other legislation he signed over two presidencies, to judge by the encouragement he received from politically and philosophically diverse newspapers nationwide. But he refused to do so, explaining that he found it unnecessarily oppressive and uncharitable, and that the qualities of a prospective desirable citizen were not necessarily contingent upon one's ability to read and write."[5]

A decade later, a 1907 House commission study concluded that immigrants from southern and eastern Europe had more "inborn socially inadequate qualities than northwestern Europeans."[6] Indeed, legislation on literacy requirements was passed again by the Senate in 1913, 1915, and 1917, only to be repeatedly vetoed by Presidents William Howard Taft and Woodrow Wilson. Congress finally had enough votes to override a veto in 1917. The law stipulated that immigrants over the age of sixteen should be able to read in at least one language. This long-debated admittance test ended up having little effect in practice; from 1920 to 1921, only about 1,450 immigrants out of more than 800,000 were barred from entering because they failed the literacy test.[7]

The first quantitative restrictions on immigration were passed by

Congress in the form of the Immigration Act of 1921, followed by the more stringent Immigration Act of 1924. The 1924 law limited the number of immigrants from any country to 2 percent of the number of people from that country already living in the United States in 1890. By using 1890 as the base year for the quotas, the law had the purposeful effect of reducing the number of immigrants from southern and eastern Europe, who came to this country in large numbers especially after that time. The law did specify that the base year for the national-origin quotas would be changed to 1920 beginning in 1927 (later postponed until 1929). The legislation further tightened the exclusion of Asian immigrants, though it continued the practice of setting no limits on immigration from countries in the Americas.

There were historically low levels of immigration to the United States in the 1930s. The Great Depression, which produced unemployment rates as high as 25 percent in 1933, made this a poor time to search for job opportunities. In some of the worst years of the Depression (1932–35), more people emigrated from, than immigrated to, the United States.[8]

After World War II, immigration policy generally became less restrictive. Many inside and outside of President Harry Truman's administration felt that for the United States to be perceived as a beacon of freedom and democracy—in contrast to its cold war rival, the Soviet Union—it needed to revise its overtly discriminatory policies.[9] While Truman advocated doing away with the national quota system, he could not muster enough support in Congress. The 1952 McCarran-Walter Immigration and Nationality Act kept the quotas largely intact but slightly liberalized immigration laws by broadening family reunification provisions; it also included separate immigrant categories for skilled workers and refugees.

The Bracero Program, initiated during a period of labor shortages during World War II, increased the number of immigrants from Mexico in the 1940s, 1950s, and 1960s. It was designed as a temporary-worker program in which Mexican workers would receive a specified minimum wage and certain working conditions. The jobs were mainly agricultural and concentrated in California, though some immigrants were brought in to work on railroad construction in a number of states. Conditions were often poor for the workers, who had relatively little power to do much about them. The Bracero Program ended in 1964.[10]

It was in 1965 that Amendments to the Immigration and Nationality Act (collectively known as the Hart-Celler Act) fundamentally revised immigration policy. This legislation eliminated the discriminatory national quota system that favored northern and western Europeans and instead allowed an annual quota of 20,000 immigrants from any country outside of the Americas, with a total cap of 170,000 annually. For the first time, a cap was placed on the number of immigrants from the Americas, at 120,000 annually. Amendments in later years brought the Americas under the same regime of uniform country quotas that applied to other regions. While there was a global ceiling of 290,000 immigrants annually, the actual number arriving has always been much greater. People exempt from quotas include spouses and unmarried minor children and parents of U.S. citizens, as well as refugees and other smaller categories of immigrants. Thus, in 1980 for example, there were about 289,000 immigrants who were subject to numerical limitation, but another 550,000 immigrants were legally admitted as close relatives of U.S. residents or as refugees.[11] In 2006, about 40 percent of the nearly 1.27 million people who gained legal permanent resident status were immediate relatives of U.S. citizens who were exempt from the numerical quotas.[12]

Perhaps the most profound effect of the 1965 Hart-Celler Act was the surge of immigration from Asia that followed. Immigration from a wide array of countries also broadened some years later, such as increased immigration from countries in Africa. The increase in immigration from Latin American countries that occurred over the same period cannot be attributed to the legislation, as the new law actually put a cap on immigration from countries in the Americas for the first time. Rather, Latin American immigration gradually increased in the

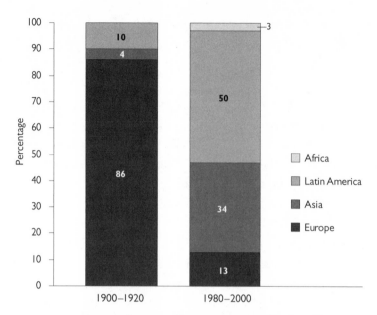

FIGURE 1. Regional origin of legal immigrants, beginning and
end of the twentieth century. Source: U.S. Immigration and
Naturalization Service (2002), *Statistical Yearbook of the Immigration and Naturalization Service, 2000* (Washington, D.C.:
U.S. Government Printing Office).

post–World War II period, and this increase continued through the
1960s and the decades after.[13]

Both changes in immigration policy and secular trends in immigration since the 1960s have had a major effect on the racial and ethnic
diversity of the American population and the distribution of minorities across the United States. Figure 1 illustrates the regional origin of
legal immigrants at the beginning and end of the twentieth century.
In the 1980–2000 period, 13 percent of all legal immigrants were from
Europe, down from 86 percent in the 1900–1920 period. The share
of immigrants from Asia grew from 4 to 34 percent, and from Latin
America from 10 to 50 percent. While the proportion of immigrants
from Africa in the 1980–2000 period was relatively small (3 percent),

the number of African immigrants has nevertheless been growing rapidly in recent years.[14]

CONTEMPORARY REGIONAL SETTLEMENT PATTERNS OF IMMIGRANTS

Alejandro Portes and Ruben Rumbaut describe how the settlement pattern of immigrants "combines two apparently contradictory outcomes: *concentration*, because a few states and metropolitan areas receive a disproportionate number of the newcomers; and *diffusion*, because immigrants are found in every state and because different immigrant types vary significantly in their locational decisions" (emphasis added).[15]

Indeed, in 2005, of the 35.7 million immigrants in the United States, about 27 percent lived in California. New York contained another 11.2 percent, followed by Texas at 9.9 percent. Florida, Illinois, and New Jersey together had another 18.4 percent, indicating that nearly two-thirds of all immigrants lived in just six states in 2005.[16] Portes and Rumbaut note that different immigrant groups often concentrate in different areas. Cubans overwhelmingly live in South Florida, Dominicans in New York and New Jersey, and Vietnamese in California.[17]

Despite this concentration, there has been a distinct shift since 1990 in the destinations of immigrants. According to Audrey Singer, by 2000 many states with few previous immigrants were experiencing rapidly growing immigrant populations. These included Colorado, Georgia, Nevada, and North Carolina. Because of their healthy economies, many emerging immigrant destinations underwent rapid growth in their native-born populations as well. Singer observes that "for the first time in recent decades it appears the dominance of California as a destination is beginning to wane as new states absorb more immigrants, including many that have never attracted many immigrants."[18]

Among metropolitan areas, emerging immigrant destinations include Atlanta, Dallas, Las Vegas, Orlando, and Washington, D.C.[19] In a study of regional changes in ethnic diversity in the years after 2000 (which did not specifically focus on immigrants), William Frey found that in 2004 Los Angeles and New York City contained 23 percent of the nation's Hispanic population, down from 30 percent in 1990. Frey also noted that the shift of the African American population from the Northeast and Midwest toward the South was accelerating—56 percent of African Americans now reside in the South.[20]

Even many small metropolitan areas are now receiving immigrants. The Greensboro–Winston-Salem–High Point metropolitan area in North Carolina, for example, has experienced tremendous growth in the number of Hispanic immigrants, who are attracted to the robust labor market, with jobs not only in agriculture but also in manufacturing, construction, and services. During the 1980s and 1990s there was also an influx of African and Asian refugees from countries such as Sudan, Somalia, Laos, and Cambodia.[21]

Suburbanization among all immigrant and racial and ethnic groups also continues. While a higher proportion of whites live in the suburbs than do other groups (more than 70 percent of non-Hispanic whites lived in suburbs in 2000), Hispanics and African Americans have suburbanized at a more rapid pace since 1990. In 2000, racial and ethnic minorities made up 27 percent of the suburban population in the 102 largest metropolitan areas, up from 19 percent in 1990.[22] As of 2000, nearly 40 percent of African Americans lived in suburbs, while nearly 50 percent of Hispanics and 55 percent of Asians lived there as well.[23]

These trends are illustrated by what is occurring in the Washington, D.C., metropolitan area. While the city has historically not been an immigration magnet, between 1980 and 2000 almost 600,000 new immigrants settled in the area. In 2000, immigrants constituted 17 percent of the metropolitan area's population, making it the seventh-largest receiving area of immigrants.[24] By 2005, the share of the D.C. metropolitan area that was foreign-born had risen to 20 percent (or more than 1 million foreign-born residents).[25] As I discuss in greater detail in following chapters, the immigrant population in D.C. is very diverse, with significant numbers from nearly all global regions—Latin

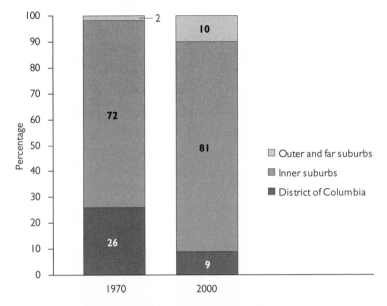

FIGURE 2. Distribution of foreign-born by area in the Washington, D.C., metropolitan area, 1970–2000. Source: Audrey Singer (2003), *At Home in the Nation's Capital: Immigrant Trends in Metropolitan Washington* (Washington, D.C.: Brookings Institution Center on Urban and Metropolitan Policy, Greater Washington Research Program, June).

America and the Caribbean, Asia, Europe, and Africa. As figure 2 illustrates, a large and growing number of the foreign-born are settling in the suburbs, even in the outer suburbs.[26]

PATTERNS OF RESIDENTIAL SEGREGATION

Immigrants are clearly moving outward from traditional immigrant destinations, but this does not necessarily mean they are living in the same communities with other groups. Over the years, researchers have developed many different measures of segregation that tap into different dimensions of residential segregation to analyze the extent to which groups share neighborhoods with each other. Douglas Massey and Nancy Denton, in an influential 1988 journal article, identified twenty such measures and classified them into five dimensions of segregation: evenness, exposure, concentration, centralization, and clustering.[27]

Evenness measures how uniformly people are distributed across neighborhoods in a metropolitan area; if the metropolitan area were, for example, 20 percent black, then each neighborhood would be 20 percent black if no segregation were present. Other measures capture *exposure*. If a group's members, for example, live in mostly homogeneous neighborhoods, then exposure to other groups is low. *Concentration* refers to population density and the amount of physical space occupied by groups, *centralization* indicates the distance from where a group lives to the center of an urban area, and *clustering* measures the degree to which group members live in neighborhoods that adjoin one another.

Segregation measurement techniques continue to evolve, propelled in part by advances in geographic information system (GIS) software that allows easier computation of complex measures of neighborhood-level settlement patterns. One more recent study has suggested that there are two primary conceptual dimensions to segregation rather than five, consisting of spatial exposure and spatial evenness.[28]

Much of my analysis relies on the two most commonly used segregation measures—dissimilarity and isolation—though at times I refer to other measures. The *dissimilarity index* is a measure of evenness, and it ranges from 0 (complete integration) to 1 (complete segregation). It describes the proportion of a group's population that would have to change residence for each neighborhood to have the same racial/ethnic distribution as the metropolitan area overall. A common rule of thumb is that dissimilarity scores of more than 0.6 are high, those from 0.3 to 0.6 are moderate, and those below 0.3 are low. The *isolation index* is a measure of exposure and also ranges from 0 to 1, with 1 indicating the highest level of isolation. It indicates the average percentage of group members (of the group of interest) in the neighborhood where the typical group member lives.

The dissimilarity index has the advantage of not being sensitive to the relative size of the groups in question. It merely provides information on how evenly members of groups are distributed across neighborhoods—however many there may be in the metropolitan area as a whole. In contrast, the isolation index is sensitive to the relative size of the groups being studied. Other factors being equal, larger ethnic groups will be more isolated from other groups than smaller ones simply because there are more coethnics present with which to share neighborhoods. This is not necessarily a negative feature of the index; from a sociological point of view, for example, it is useful to know how much potential contact there is between groups. Appendix A provides a detailed discussion of issues involved in measuring residential segregation and a description of how alternative measures are calculated.

Trends in Segregation by Race and Ethnicity, 1980–2000

In 2002, the U.S. Census Bureau released a report titled *Racial and Ethnic Residential Segregation in the United States: 1980–2000* (which I coauthored).[29] Its major findings were as follows:

- Declines in black-white metropolitan segregation over the 1980–2000 period occurred across all five dimensions of residential segregation considered.
- Despite these declines, residential segregation was still higher for African Americans than for the other groups across all measures. Hispanics were generally the next most highly segregated from non-Hispanic whites, followed by Asians.
- Asians, as well as Hispanics, tended to experience increases in segregation from whites over the period, though this depended on the measure used.

Figure 3 illustrates these findings. First, we see that the average black-white dissimilarity score averaged across all U.S. metropoli-

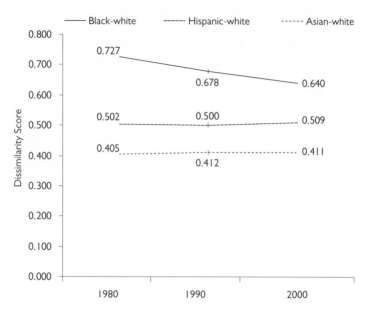

FIGURE 3. Dissimilarity scores by race, Hispanic origin, and year, 1980–2000. Source: John Iceland, Daniel H. Weinberg, and Erika Steinmetz (2002), *Racial and Ethnic Residential Segregation in the United States: 1980–2000*, U.S. Census Bureau, Census Special Report, CENSR-3 (Washington, D.C.: U.S. Government Printing Office). Note: Scores represent weighted averages for all metropolitan areas.

tan areas declined from 0.727 in 1980 to 0.640 in 2000.[30] The 0.640 figure can be interpreted as indicating that about 64 percent of African Americans (or whites) would have to move for all neighborhoods in the metropolitan area to have an equal proportion of African Americans (or whites). Hispanic-white dissimilarity increased very slightly from 0.502 to 0.509 over the same period, while the scores for Asians likewise increased slightly, from 0.405 to 0.411. Thus, while black-white dissimilarity dropped by 12.0 percent from 1980 to 2000, Hispanic-white dissimilarity increased by 1.4 percent and Asian-white dissimilarity increased by 1.5 percent over the period.

Figure 4 shows trends in isolation. Black isolation declined moder-

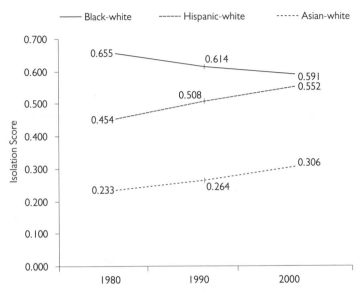

FIGURE 4. Isolation scores by race, Hispanic origin, and year, 1980–2000. Source: John Iceland, Daniel H. Weinberg, and Erika Steinmetz (2002), *Racial and Ethnic Residential Segregation in the United States: 1980–2000*, U.S. Census Bureau, Census Special Report, CENSR-3 (Washington, D.C.: U.S. Government Printing Office). Note: Scores represent weighted averages for all metropolitan areas.

ately over the period, from 0.655 to 0.591. The 0.591 figure indicates that the typical African American lived in a neighborhood that was on average 59 percent African American in 2000. In contrast, Hispanic isolation increased significantly, from 0.454 in 1980 to 0.552 in 2000, so that by the latter year Hispanic isolation was approaching black isolation levels. Asian isolation also increased, though from relatively low levels. In 2000, the Asian isolation index was 0.306. Higher isolation in 2000 than in previous decades indicates that Asians and Hispanics were living in neighborhoods that contained a higher proportion of Asians and Hispanics in 2000, respectively, than in 1980. As the Hispanic and Asian population continues to grows, we will likely see further increases in isolation in the future, even if these groups remain about as evenly distributed as before (as indicated by the dissimilarity index).

These findings have several implications for residential patterns in metropolitan America. First, they indicate that black-white segregation continues to be quite high in absolute terms. These high levels lend credence to the ethnic disadvantage (or place stratification) perspective on residential patterns. As described in the previous chapter, these perspectives emphasize the role of discrimination and related forces in shaping residential patterns. A number of researchers documented the rise of the American ghetto in the twentieth century when African Americans migrated to northern inner cities in large numbers. Even as formal barriers to integration fell in the civil rights era, the legacy of past discrimination and segregation and continued racism likely help explain high levels of segregation between African Americans and whites today.[31]

Indeed, larger metropolitan areas in the Midwest and Northeast have among the highest levels of black-white segregation, while newer metropolitan areas with smaller black populations in the South and West tend to be less segregated. Among large metropolitan areas with a sizable African American presence, the five most segregated in 2000, as shown by the dissimilarity index, were Detroit, Milwaukee, New York, Newark, and Chicago. The five least segregated of these large metropolitan areas were Orange County, San Jose, Phoenix-Mesa, Riverside–San Bernardino, and Norfolk–Virginia Beach–Newport.[32]

Despite high levels, black-white segregation declined significantly over the 1980–2000 period. This trend is consistent with research showing an increased willingness by whites to remain in their neighborhoods as African Americans enter.[33] Certainly, over the years, formal barriers to integration have fallen with the passage of various laws, including the Fair Housing Act of 1968. This legislation made it unlawful to discriminate on the basis of race, color, religion, or national origin in most housing market transactions. Amendments to the act in 1988 strengthened its enforcement. Research has indicated that discrimination in rental and owner-occupied housing markets indeed declined substantially in the 1990s, though discrimination still occurs. In their study of these issues, Stephen Ross and Margery Turner conclude that declines in discrimination are probably a result of changing attitudes in society, increased contact of real-estate agents with minority customers, the continuing effect of the Fair Housing Act on the real-estate industry and the law's enforcement, and the rising socioeconomic status of minority customers.[34]

Regional patterns of migration also indicate that newer metropolitan areas in the South are gaining in their black populations relative to Rust Belt cities with sizable ghettos in the Northeast and Midwest. For example, the metropolitan areas with the largest absolute gains in black population from 2000 to 2004 were Atlanta, Miami, Dallas, Washington, D.C., and Houston.[35] Moreover, metropolitan areas that had the largest percentage increases in their black populations from 1980 to 2000 registered larger declines in black-white dissimilarity than those with the slowest black population growth.[36] This suggests that the hypersegregation between blacks and whites that characterized many older industrial centers of the Northeast and Midwest is not, thus far, being reproduced in high-growth metropolitan areas in the South and West.

Increases in Hispanic segregation from other groups in the 1980–2000 period were most evident in metropolitan areas experiencing rapid increases in their Hispanic population. For example, Atlanta, dubbed a "new Hispanic destination," recorded a 56 percent increase in Hispanic segregation from other groups (though overall levels are still moderate)—even as black segregation in the metropolitan area declined. This suggests that the arrival of new immigrants, who are often apt to settle in ethnic enclaves, is playing a role in shaping these residential patterns.[37] This issue is examined in more detail in the following two chapters.

Residential Segregation and Socioeconomic Status

The question about the potential role of groups' average socioeconomic status (SES) in explaining residential patterns is an important one. One of the central tenets of the spatial assimilation perspective is that even if there were no prejudice and discrimination affecting people's residential choices, there would, theoretically, be considerable segregation if the average incomes of groups differed. In the U.S. context, such differences could mean that minority members may simply be unable to afford to live in the same neighborhoods as more affluent whites. The poor may be more likely to live in distinct areas, such as central cities, where public transport is more readily available and government support more generous.[38]

African Americans and Hispanics in particular lag behind whites in terms of income, occupational status, and education. For example, in 2005, the median household income of non-Hispanic whites, at $50,784, was considerably higher than that of blacks ($30,858) and Hispanics ($35,967), though lower than that of Asians ($61,094).[39] A higher proportion of non-Hispanic whites had advanced college degrees and were managers than blacks and Hispanics, though this proportion was again lower than that observed among Asians.[40] Similarly, African American and Hispanic poverty rates in 2005 (24.9 and 21.8 percent, respectively) were roughly three times higher than that of non-Hispanic whites (8.3 percent); the Asian poverty rate (11.1 percent) was also moderately higher than that of whites.[41]

According to the spatial assimilation perspective, individuals who achieve socioeconomic gains, however, should be able to translate these gains into higher-quality neighborhoods and housing; such neighborhoods also often have a higher proportion of white residents. Figure 5 illustrates patterns of residential segregation by race and Hispanic origin and approximate household income quartiles using the dissimilarity index in 2000.[42] That is, the figure shows how segregated blacks, Hispanics, and Asians in four different (and roughly equal) income

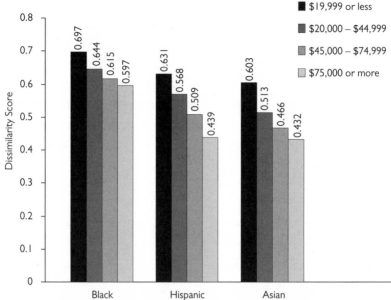

FIGURE 5. Dissimilarity from non-Hispanic whites by race/ethnicity and income quartile, 2000. Source: John Iceland and Rima Wilkes (2006), "Does Socioeconomic Status Matter? Race, Class, and Residential Segregation," *Social Problems* 52, 2:248–73.

categories were from non-Hispanic whites. A central finding is that higher-income blacks, Hispanics, and Asians were all less segregated from non-Hispanic whites than were their lower-income counterparts. For example, the dissimilarity score of African Americans in the lowest household income quartile (0.697) was appreciably higher than the score in the highest income quartile (0.597). However, it is important to point out that even among high-income African Americans, segregation was virtually at the level generally recognized as being high in absolute terms (0.6).[43]

We also see lower Hispanic-white segregation among higher-income Hispanics. For example, the dissimilarity score among Hispanics in the lowest income quartile was 0.631, considerably higher than the 0.439 score among those in the top income quartile. Likewise, the dissimilarity score for Asians in the lowest income quartile (0.603) was also significantly higher than among the highest-quartile Asian households (0.432). Overall, we see that differences in the segregation of low- and high-income Hispanics from whites (43.7 percent difference in dissimilarity scores) and low- and high-income Asians (39.6 percent difference) from whites are larger than the difference observed among low- and high-income blacks (16.8 percent difference). This suggests that the spatial assimilation model explains better the Hispanic and Asian segregation patterns from non-Hispanic whites than those of African Americans.

These patterns are also consistent with previous research on these issues. For example, in a study of segregation patterns in immigrant gateway cities, William Clark and Sarah Blue found that blacks, Asians, and Hispanics with high educational levels and incomes were less segregated from whites than those with low levels of education and income—particularly in the suburbs.[44]

It is important to note that the role of income in influencing black-white levels of segregation has increased in recent years. For example, the black-white dissimilarity score for blacks in the highest income quartile was 0.597 in 2000, down from 0.620 in 1990. Yet among low-income blacks in the lowest quartile, segregation from whites actually increased a bit from 0.671 to 0.697 over the same period. Overall, this suggests that the importance of socioeconomic status in shaping African American residential patterns is increasing, though in 2000 this effect was still not as great as witnessed among Hispanics and Asians.[45]

Convergence in Patterns by Race and Ethnicity?

In a recent paper, Jeffrey Timberlake and I examined patterns of residential inequality from 1970 to 2000 by race and Hispanic origin using several measures of residential inequality.[46] In addition to the dissimilarity and isolation indexes mentioned above, we also looked at patterns using the multigroup *information theory index* (also known as the entropy index, or Theil's H). This index has the advantage of summarizing the segregation of multiple groups from each other, rather than simply looking at the segregation of pairs of groups as is typically done with the dissimilarity and isolation indexes. We also used the *net difference index*. This measure is not a conventional segregation measure per se but rather a measure of the extent to which one group is concentrated in more disadvantaged (poorer) neighborhoods than another group. The net difference measure complements the other measures because it more directly measures locational attainment, that is, the extent to which some groups live in poorer neighborhoods than do other groups.[47]

Our analysis yielded several conclusions. First, the residential segregation between all four groups (whites, blacks, Hispanics, and Asians) declined substantially over the 1970–2000 period, as indicated by the multigroup entropy index (findings using this index are discussed in more detail in chapter 6). Second, consistent with findings reported in figures 3 and 4, white-black residential segregation and inequality had declined substantially since 1970 using all indexes. The extreme levels of residential inequality that blacks uniquely suffered throughout much of the twentieth century are thus converging with the inequality experienced by Hispanics and, to a lesser extent, Asians.[48]

Third, we found that this convergence was especially pronounced with the index of net difference. In 1970, the probability that a randomly selected African American would live in a poorer neighborhood than a randomly selected white person was 65 percent greater than the reverse probability; for Hispanics, the difference in these probabilities was only about 27 percent. By 2000, black-white net difference was down to 50 percent, and the Hispanic-white net difference was up to 39 percent. Thus, the black/Hispanic gap in net differences had declined to about 11 percentage points in 2000, meaning that blacks and Hispanics shared nearly equivalent levels of neighborhood disadvantage (at least in terms of neighborhood poverty rates) relative to whites.

Consistent with other research, we also found that although Asians were living in more ethnically concentrated neighborhoods over time, as indicated by the isolation index, they were not living in neighborhoods with increasingly higher poverty rates relative to whites. Sociologist John Logan and his colleagues have argued that this finding may be explained by the tendency of Asian immigrants, often with relatively high income levels, to settle in "ethnic communities" in American suburbs with moderately high percentages of Asian residents.[49]

Fourth, we found that lower levels of income inequality between whites and the three minority groups were strongly associated with lower levels of residential inequality, consistent with the predictions of spatial assimilation theory. That is, blacks and Hispanics in particular convert economic gains into reductions in residential disadvantage. It is noteworthy that the effects of income equality are not as strong in predicting reductions in the three indexes of residential segregation (as opposed to disadvantage) for either group. We concluded that rising incomes for blacks and Hispanics relative to whites are converted into improved neighborhood conditions a little more so than increased residential integration with whites.

Finally, we found that if 1970–2000 trends continue, Hispanics will overtake blacks as the most segregated racial/ethnic group by soon after the year 2010, though any such projection should be viewed with caution, given the unpredictability of these types of trends.

On the whole, it is difficult to say whether the convergence of black and Hispanic residential patterns represents good or bad news. On the one hand, recent trends indicate that white resistance to living with African Americans has continued to erode over time. Given that whites have not typically shown the same antipathy toward Hispanics as toward blacks, we speculated that increases in Hispanic segregation might turn out to be fueled mostly by high levels of immigration, and therefore rather short-lived, given past moderate assimilation of Hispanics into American society.[50] On the other hand, the rather rapid increases in Hispanic isolation, both in central-city locations and inner-ring suburbs, could indicate that new, more permanent ethnic enclaves could be taking root in many metropolitan areas.[51] I investigate these issues further in the following two chapters.

CONCLUSIONS

On the whole, this analysis of trends in residential segregation suggests that there have been some important changes in the extent of "American Apartheid" in U.S. metropolitan areas, as powerfully described by Douglas Massey and Nancy Denton in their book of the early 1990s (which relied on data from 1980 and earlier).[52] One of these changes is that while African Americans continue to face important constraints in their housing choices, they are more likely to realize their residential choices than in previous decades.

In the early decades of the twentieth century, residential color lines were often enforced through violence directed at individual blacks who "trespassed" into white neighborhoods, such as in race riots in New York City, East St. Louis, and Chicago. Even in the post–World War II period, the ghetto was maintained by discrimination by real-estate agents and in the mortgage industry. Many real-estate agents, often acting on the preferences of their white clients, simply refused to sell blacks property in white neighborhoods, and blacks had difficulty obtaining loans for buying houses. In communities that adopted restrictive covenants, individuals were also legally prohibited from selling their homes to blacks.[53] Violence and intimidation directed at blacks were common. Today, discrimination is more likely to take the form of real-estate agents steering different ethnic groups toward different neighborhoods, minorities being shown fewer properties than white home seekers, and some differences in the ease of obtaining loans. Discrimination is generally less overt, and many would argue that it is less prevalent and virulent than in the past.

Among people who study and write about these issues, there are of course differences of opinion on the state of race relations in the United

States. On the one hand, there is overwhelming evidence suggesting the continuing salience of racial and ethnic stratification in American society. With non-Hispanic whites still in control of many levers of power, it is more often minority groups, and African Americans in particular, who find themselves facing constraints in their efforts to achieve upward mobility. Black and Hispanic incomes lag far behind those of whites and Asians, and inequality is even greater when one considers wealth rather than income.[54] The plight of young black men is often highlighted in both academic work and the popular press because of continued high levels of unemployment and incarceration among this demographic group.[55]

Nevertheless, there has been a slow, if not always steady, decline in black disadvantage over the past few decades. This extends to trends in poverty, education, income, wealth, and, the focus here, residential circumstances.[56] Because the foundations of what Massey and Denton called American Apartheid are deep-rooted, however, it will still take decades to redress inequality at the current pace of change.

Another central conclusion of this chapter is that part of the convergence in residential patterns described for all groups is actually a result of increases in Hispanic-white and Asian-white segregation along some (though not all) dimensions of segregation. The question remains whether these results indicate increasing ethnic polarization and social distance between whites and Hispanics and Asians. The alternative explanation is that increasing levels of segregation are in part a function of the fact that continued immigration translates into a growth in ethnic enclaves, at least in the short run. If so, the spatial assimilation model would predict that segregation is lower for both the native-born of these groups and those with greater socioeconomic resources who can translate their status into better—and perhaps more integrated—housing. The analysis thus far has indicated that socioeconomic status is indeed an important predictor of segregation. The next chapter therefore focuses on the role of immigration in explaining recent increases in Hispanic-white and Asian-white segregation.

CHAPTER 4

Immigrant Residential Segregation

In 2007 the Associated Press reported that Sunnyslope, one of Phoenix, Arizona's, oldest neighborhoods, was being transformed by immigration.[1] Over the prior decade, so many immigrants from the state of Oaxaca in Mexico had moved to the area that it was becoming known as "Little Oaxaca." The story recounted that "waves of Mexican immigrants fleeing poverty in Oaxaca are drawn to Sunnyslope for its affordable housing and its access to major bus routes, which provide quick rides to jobs throughout the city [of Phoenix]. . . . They are transforming pockets of the neighborhood, and re-creating pieces of the Mexican villages they left behind."

Why were so many immigrants from Oaxaca congregating in the same community north of the border? "Everyone here in this neighborhood is going through the same thing," Rogelio, a day laborer, told the reporter. "You miss your family, your country. The greenness of everything down there (in Oaxaca). The good thing is, you can always find someone from Oaxaca around here to talk to about it. They're everywhere."

Naturally, the experts also weighed in: "The neighborhoods help cushion immigrants' adjustment to the U.S. . . . and allow them to still feel close to their homelands," reported the Associated Press, citing experts. "Earlier immigrants help recent immigrants navigate, introducing them to people in the neighborhood, showing them how the bus system works and connecting them to priests and churches."

It has long been conventional wisdom that new immigrants often prefer to settle in ethnic enclaves populated by people who share their common history and culture. Living among friends and family can bring comfort in a place where many seemingly simple transactions can be bewilderingly complex. What is less clear, however, is whether and to what extent immigrants are more likely to move out of these enclaves the longer they are in the host country, and whether this movement outward is all the more true among their children. One might think that since ethnicity plays a large role in the organization of urban space in the United States, it would likewise affect the settlement decisions of immigrants and subsequent generations. The purpose of this chapter is to therefore gauge the levels of residential segregation of immigrants and the extent to which race, ethnicity, the length of time in the United States, and socioeconomic characteristics shape these patterns.

The analysis here is guided by the following specific questions: (1) Are foreign-born Hispanics, Asians, and blacks more segregated from non-Hispanic whites than the native-born of those respective groups? (2) Are immigrants who have been in the United States for shorter periods of time more segregated from non-Hispanic whites than less recent arrivals? (3) Are residential patterns in large part explained by the characteristics of immigrants, such as socioeconomic status and other acculturation indicators (such as English-language fluency)?

An answer of "yes" to all of these questions would provide strong support for the notion that immigrants are spatially assimilating. A set of "yes" answers for some immigrant groups, such as Hispanics and Asians, but not for others, such as blacks, would suggest that the segmented assimilation perspective discussed in chapter 2 may provide a better framework for understanding immigrant patterns of incorporation. That is, while some groups are exhibiting traditional patterns of assimilation with the non-Hispanic whites, other groups are not. Finally, if there is little relation between segregation and nativity and length of time in the United States among any racial or ethnic group, then the ethnic disadvantage (or place stratification) approach receives the strongest support. That is, assimilation is not the prevalent pattern and immigrants and the subsequent generations are maintaining their ethnic neighborhoods.

Much of the following analysis draws upon 1990 and 2000 census data. I examine residential patterns using the dissimilarity index, which is a measure of how evenly different groups are distributed across neighborhoods in a metropolitan area. Detailed tabulations with both the dissimilarity and isolation indexes are included in tables B.2–B.5 in appendix B. Details about the methodology used are described in appendix A.[2]

The findings presented here provide general support for the spatial assimilation perspective, particularly for Hispanics and Asians. While some patterns are consistent with spatial assimilation among black immigrants, the overall very high levels of segregation of black immigrants tend to overshadow all else and thus provide some support for the segmented assimilation perspective—that patterns of incorporation differ across immigrant groups.

RESIDENTIAL SEGREGATION BY NATIVITY,
YEAR OF ENTRY, AND RACE AND ETHNICITY

Figure 6 shows average levels of metropolitan residential segregation of the foreign-born from native-born non-Hispanic whites by year-of-entry cohort and census year.[3] The first two columns in figure 6 shows that between 1990 and 2000, the overall dissimilarity score rose modestly, from 0.411 to 0.443, suggesting increasing segregation of the foreign-born from native-born non-Hispanic whites over that ten-year period. However, subsequent columns illustrate two patterns: (1) more-recent arrivals had higher levels of segregation than those who immigrated much earlier according to either 1990 or 2000 census data,

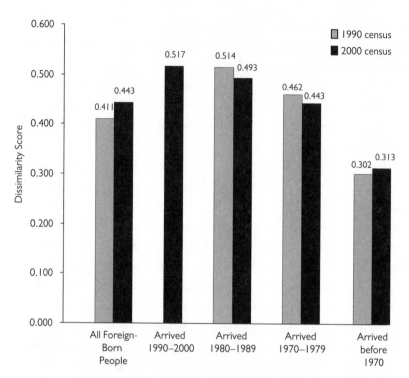

FIGURE 6. Dissimilarity of the foreign-born from native-born non-Hispanic whites by year-of-entry cohort and census year, 1990 and 2000. Source: John Iceland and Melissa Scopilliti (2008), "Immigrant Residential Segregation in U.S. Metropolitan Areas, 1990–2000," *Demography* 45, 1:79–94.

and (2) segregation for approximate year-of-entry cohorts also declined modestly from 1990 to 2000, except for pre-1970 arrivals. Both of these general findings support the spatial assimilation model.

Illustrating the first finding, we see that, according to 2000 census figures, the dissimilarity score for the foreign-born who arrived between 1990 and 2000 was 0.517, though it was only 0.313 for immigrants who arrived before 1970. Illustrating the second pattern, we see that the dissimilarity score for those who arrived between 1980 and 1989 was 0.493 in 2000, down from 0.514 in 1990, indicating a modest decline in segregation for a particular year-of-entry cohort over time. The one exception is for those immigrants who arrived before 1970, where the change in the dissimilarity score was not statistically significant. It should be noted that the data from 1990 and 2000 do not follow true cohorts, only approximate ones. That is, some of the immigrants who were counted in 1990 were no longer in the United States in 2000 (as a result of emigration or death).[4] In both census years there may of course be some misreporting about timing of immigration.

Table 1 provides further detail by showing average levels of metropolitan residential segregation by race and ethnicity. Among Hispanics and Asians as whole, we see a pattern of little change in dissimilarity from native-born non-Hispanic whites (at times termed more simply as *whites* below) from the 1990 census to 2000. However, we also see that among all racial and ethnic groups, the foreign-born are more segregated from whites than the native-born of these groups. This finding is again consistent with the predictions of spatial assimilation theory. As with findings for the foreign-born as a whole, we see that recent Hispanic and Asian immigrants tend to have higher levels of segregation from whites than Hispanics and Asians who have been in the United States longer. Segregation declined modestly for most cohorts of Hispanics in the ten years between the 1990 and 2000 censuses, though changes for Asians are not statistically significant. Hispanic-white segregation is generally higher than Asian-white segregation.

The pattern for foreign-born blacks differs in some important respects from that of Hispanics and Asians. We see that the segregation from whites of all blacks, native-born blacks, and foreign-born blacks generally declined between the 1990 and 2000 censuses, in contrast to the trend for Hispanics and Asians, where declines for these general groups were not the norm. However, when we look at data from either census, more-recent arrivals do not have higher dissimilarity scores than earlier arrivals. In addition, the small declines in dissimilarity for cohorts from 1990 to 2000 are not statistically significant. These latter findings are not consistent with spatial assimilation.

TABLE I. Dissimilarity from Native-Born Non-Hispanic Whites by
Race, Hispanic Origin, and Nativity, and Year of Entry, 1990 and 2000

	Number of Metropolitan Areas	1990	2000
All foreign-born people	**187**	**0.411**	**0.443**
1990–2000	187	—	0.517
1980–1989	187	0.514	0.493
1970–1979	187	0.462	0.443
Before 1970	187	0.302	0.313
All Hispanics	**170**	**0.514**	**0.522**
Native-born	170	0.480	0.481
Foreign-born	170	0.598	0.599
All foreign-born Hispanics	84	0.600	0.602
1990–2000	84	—	0.651
1980–1989	84	0.650	0.623
1970–1979	84	0.628	0.600
Before 1970	84	0.530	0.514
All Asians and Pacific Islanders	**157**	**0.434**	**0.434**
Native-born	157	0.402	0.394
Foreign-born	157	0.475	0.477
All foreign-born Asians and Pacific Islanders	63	0.475	0.482
1990–2000	63	—	0.545
1980–1989	63	0.534	0.520
1970–1979	63	0.484	0.475
Before 1970	63	0.498	0.507
All blacks	**84**	**0.713**	**0.674**
Native-born	84	0.716	0.675
Foreign-born	84	0.747	0.712
All foreign-born blacks	24	0.754	0.727
1990–2000	24	—	0.751

TABLE I *(continued)*

	Number of Metropolitan Areas	1990	2000
1980–1989	24	0.775	0.751
1970–1979	24	0.778	0.754
Before 1970	24	0.784	0.772
Foreign-born non-Hispanic whites	**91**	**0.271**	**0.305**
1990–2000	91	—	0.470
1980–1989	91	0.451	0.420
1970–1979	91	0.408	0.403
Before 1970	91	0.247	0.270

SOURCE: John Iceland and Melissa Scopilliti, "Immigrant Residential Segregation in U.S. Metropolitan Areas, 1990–2000," *Demography* 45, 1:79–94.

NOTE: Includes metropolitan areas with at least 1,000 members of the group in question in 1990 and 2000. Means are weighted by the size of the group in question. Higher values indicate more segregation. Metropolitan areas held constant for all year-of-entry categories within each ethnic grouping to facilitate comparison across these categories.

The pattern for foreign-born non-Hispanic whites is actually quite similar to patterns for Hispanic and Asian immigrants, though the overall level of segregation for this group from native-born non-Hispanic whites is appreciably lower. More-recent white immigrants have higher levels of segregation than those who have been in the United States longer. We also see declines in segregation for the recent cohort, though little change for those who came from 1970 to 1979 and actual increases among those arriving before 1970. That segregation increased between 1990 and 2000 for those who entered the United States before 1970 could reflect a compositional change in that group: in 1990, a higher proportion of those immigrants came from the pre-1920s immigration boom, whereas by 2000 a number of those immigrants had died and the population therefore consisted more of immigrants who arrived in later years.

Overall, these figures provide some support for the spatial assimilation perspective, though a few patterns are equivocal and there is some variation across racial and ethnic groups. Certainly, spatial assimilation appears to be less prevalent among black immigrants than among other groups, and foreign-born whites display the lowest levels of segregation from native-born non-Hispanic whites compared to other groups.

Case Study: Washington, D.C.

Despite a number of unique features of the Washington, D.C., metropolitan area, the residential patterns that characterize metropolitan areas across the country as a whole are clearly illustrated there. First, a few words about the demography and geography of metropolitan Washington are in order. Washington has traditionally been a black-white city. As recently as 1970, the foreign-born made up just 5 percent of the population. Today, metropolitan Washington is considered one of the largest destinations for immigrants. As of 2005, the metropolitan area had a total population of 5.1 million. About 52 percent of the population was non-Hispanic white, 27 percent African American, 8 percent Asian, 11 percent Hispanic, and 2 percent American Indian or two or more races. A full 20 percent of the people (or more than 1 million) in the metropolitan area were foreign-born. The D.C. population is on average better educated and more affluent than in the nation as a whole. More than 1 in 5 people over twenty-five years old had a graduate or professional degree, and another 25 percent had a B.A. (compared with 10 and 15 percent of the U.S. population, respectively). The median household income was $74,708 in 2005 (compared with $46,242 nationally), and only 7 percent of the population was poor (versus 13 percent nationally).[5]

Washington is also notable for having a very sizable black middle class. In fact, the median household income of blacks in the D.C. metropolitan area, at $53,686 in 2005, while certainly lower than that of non-Hispanic whites ($88,740) and Asians ($80,781), was nevertheless higher than the overall U.S. median household income ($46,242). The median household income of Hispanics ($53,906) was similar to that of blacks in the D.C. area.[6] Washington is also known for having pockets of deep poverty, and African American poverty in particular, mainly concentrated in the eastern sections of the central city, with some in the inner suburbs to the east of the city.

Declines in black-white segregation that we saw nationwide in the 1980–2000 period also occurred in metropolitan Washington. For example, the black-white dissimilarity index fell from 0.687 in 1980 to 0.625 in 2000 (see figure 7). Despite the decline, segregation remains high in absolute terms (using 0.6 as a common marker of high dissimilarity). Blacks also became less isolated and centralized over the period, the latter in large part reflecting the increased suburbanization of blacks, particularly to the east of the city (and in Prince George's County in particular). Meanwhile, Hispanic-white dissimilarity, which was at a fairly modest level in 1980 (0.322), increased substantially over the two decades, to 0.480 in 2000. Asian-white dissimilarity also increased over the period, from 0.322 to 0.382. Isolation increased to an even greater extent for both Hispanics and Asians (see figure B.2 in appendix B), also reflecting the large growth in their respective populations in the D.C. area. These increases in segregation are higher than national average changes for these groups.[7]

About 39 percent of the Washington metropolitan area's immigrants in 2005 were born in Latin America, another 36 percent in Asia, 13 percent in Africa, and 10 percent in Europe. The largest sending countries were El Salvador, with 129,000 (or 12.7 percent) of the foreign-born population, India (6.2 percent), Korea and China (5.1 percent), and Mexico (4.4 percent).[8] The metropolitan area now has thirty zip codes where more than 30 percent of the residents are foreign-born, and many of these immigrants are in the inner suburbs.[9]

Census data indicate that foreign-born Hispanics are concentrated in the inner suburbs of the Washington metropolitan area, along some of the major transportation lines extending outward from the city,

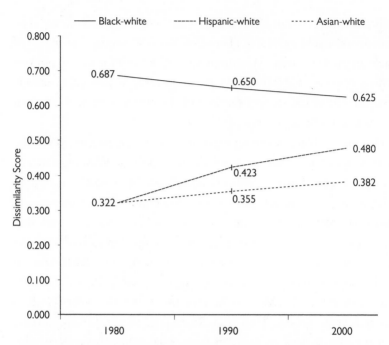

FIGURE 7. Residential segregation in Washington, D.C., by group; dissimilarity index, 1980–2000. Source: John Iceland, Daniel H. Weinberg, and Erika Steinmetz (2002), *Racial and Ethnic Residential Segregation in the United States: 1980–2000*, U.S. Census Bureau, Census Special Report, CENSR-3 (Washington, D.C.: U.S. Government Printing Office).

and also in the central part of D.C. itself. In fact, it is interesting to see how Hispanics, including foreign-born Hispanics, often seem to occupy a middle ground between whites and blacks in the city and surrounding areas—with whites to the west and blacks to the east. Non-Hispanic whites are also more likely to live in outer suburban counties than Hispanics and blacks. Overall, dissimilarity between whites and Hispanic immigrants is moderate to high at 0.56 in metropolitan Washington. Isolation, at 0.34, indicates that the typical Hispanic immigrant lives in a neighborhood where on average 34 percent of the residents are Hispanic immigrants.[10]

Asians immigrants are less segregated from native-born non-Hispanic whites than Hispanic immigrants. The dissimilarity score, at 0.43, is well within the moderate range, and isolation, at 0.19, is fairly low. Indeed, Asian immigrants are more evenly distributed across the suburbs of the Washington metropolitan area, including some of the outer suburbs. Unlike for Hispanics, there is also no particular cluster of Asian immigrants to the north and east of the city or in D.C. itself.

In contrast, there are distinct clusters of black immigrants in the eastern portion of D.C. and in the suburbs to the east. These are areas that have a large native-born African American population. Indeed, news stories in the *Washington Post* have noted that African immigrants, such as from Nigeria and Ghana, are moving to communities across Prince George's County.[11] At 0.64, the dissimilarity between black immigrants and native-born non-Hispanic whites is high, though the isolation score, at 0.30, is not. The typical black immigrant does not live in a neighborhood comprising mainly other black immigrants, in part because of the relatively small black immigrant population in the metropolitan area more generally.

The number of white immigrants is small, and they are widely distributed across metropolitan Washington. As a result, there are only moderate to low levels of dissimilarity (0.34) between native- and foreign-born whites (scores below 0.3 are generally considered low). Isolation, at 0.10, is also quite low in absolute terms.

In summary, these patterns in metropolitan Washington help illustrate the national patterns of immigrant residential segregation from native-born non-Hispanic whites: high levels among black immigrants, low levels among white immigrants, and more moderate levels among Hispanics and Asians.

Segregation by Country of Origin

Figures 8 through 11 show dissimilarity scores of the foreign-born by race and ethnicity and year of entry for selected countries of origin,

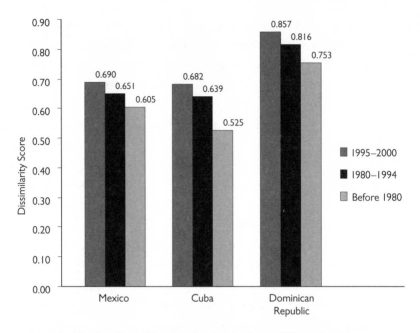

FIGURE 8. Foreign-born Hispanic/native-born non-Hispanic white dissimilarity by country of birth and year of entry, 2000. Source: Analysis of 2000 decennial census data.

where the reference group is again native-born non-Hispanic whites (tables B.2–B.5 in appendix B contain information on additional sending countries, as well as isolation scores for all groups).[12]

Figure 8 shows the dissimilarity of Hispanic immigrants from Mexico, Cuba, and the Dominican Republic from native-born non-Hispanic whites. The patterns in the figure provide general support for the spatial assimilation model, as those from all three countries who have been in the United States longer are less segregated from whites than recent arrivals. Year of entry has the greatest salience among Cuban immigrants, where long-time residents are much less segregated from whites than newcomers. We also see that overall levels of segregation from non-Hispanic whites are greater among Dominicans than among Mexicans or Cubans.

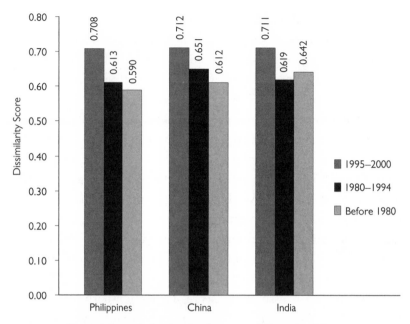

FIGURE 9. Foreign-born Asian/native-born non-Hispanic white
dissimilarity by country of birth and year of entry, 2000. Source:
Analysis of 2000 decennial census data.

In figure 9, we see similar patterns among foreign-born Asians from
selected countries—Philippines, China, and India—as we did among
Hispanic groups. Those who immigrated in the five years prior to the
census are more segregated from non-Hispanic whites than those who
arrived before 1980. In general, there is not an incredible amount of
variation across these three particular Asian countries (see appendix
table B.3 for the full list), though among Indian immigrants, for example, those who arrived before 1980 are actually more segregated from
whites than those arriving from 1980 to 1994.

The dissimilarity scores for specific Asian countries of origin in
figure 9 are actually higher than those for foreign-born Asians as a
whole (shown in table 1), indicating that specific groups often settle in
particular neighborhoods—often different neighborhoods from each
other—than Asians as a whole. That is, if, say, Chinese immigrants

settle in a few specific neighborhoods in a metropolitan area, and Indian immigrants settle in other particular neighborhoods, then each will have relatively high residential dissimilarity from whites (they are not evenly distributed across neighborhoods in a metropolitan area); but the broader group, "Asians," may end up being somewhat more evenly distributed because pan-ethnic group members are generally present in a broader array of neighborhoods than individuals from the constituent countries of origin. Indeed there is, for example, a relatively high concentration of Vietnamese immigrants in the Adams Morgan and Mt. Pleasant neighborhoods of Washington, D.C., while there is a relatively high proportion of Chinese immigrants in Gaithersburg, a suburb to the north in Maryland. Certainly, there are yet other neighborhoods that contain a significant number of Asian immigrant groups, such as Annandale, an inner suburb in Virginia.[13]

Figure 10 shows dissimilarity scores for foreign-born blacks from Jamaica, Haiti, and Nigeria.[14] The figure shows that immigrants from these three countries were extremely segregated from native-born non-Hispanic whites, with scores for all year-of-entry categories 0.789 or more. There is a slight pattern of lower segregation among Jamaican and Haitian immigrants who have been in the United States longer, but no such pattern among Nigerians. Thus, support for the spatial assimilation model is quite weak, at best, when considering foreign-born blacks.

These findings are generally in line with those from previous studies using older data. For example, using 1990 data from two metropolitan areas (Miami and New York), Lance Freeman found that foreign-born blacks who immigrated in the 1980s had about the same level of segregation as those who immigrated before 1970 in one metropolitan area, and only slightly lower segregation in the other, providing little support for the spatial assimilation model.[15] Similarly, Nancy Denton and Douglas Massey in one study and Kyle Crowder in another also concluded that race plays the most important role in explaining residential patterns of black immigrants from the Caribbean.[16] Crowder's study

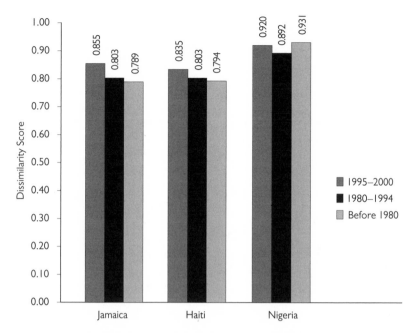

FIGURE 10. Foreign-born black/native-born non-Hispanic white dissimilarity by country of birth and year of entry, 2000. Source: Analysis of 2000 decennial census data.

indicated that despite a relatively favorable socioeconomic profile, West Indians in the New York metropolitan area in 1990 were concentrated in largely black neighborhoods. However, they often lived in ethnically distinct enclaves within black areas—often in higher-income neighborhoods—allowing them to avoid the most depressed black neighborhoods in metropolitan New York.[17]

Finally, figure 11 shows the segregation of foreign-born whites from Poland, the United Kingdom, and Germany from native-born non-Hispanic whites.[18] Dissimilarity scores tend to be high for recent arrivals, and even for those who arrived between 1980 and 1994, but considerably lower for immigrants who have been in the United States for at least twenty years. Note that many of those who have been in the country for at least twenty years likely arrived decades ago. Higher

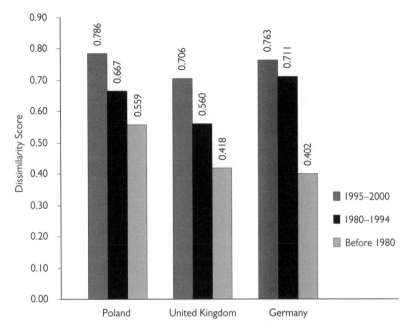

FIGURE II. Foreign-born non-Hispanic white/native-born non-Hispanic white dissimilarity by country of birth and year of entry, 2000. Source: Analysis of 2000 decennial census data.

dissimilarity scores for each of the country-of-origin groups than for overall foreign-born whites once again indicate that specific groups sometimes occupy residential niches, though foreign-born whites as a whole are fairly evenly spread across various neighborhoods. Overall, the spatial assimilation model is strongly supported by these patterns— more so than for any other immigrant group.

THE ROLE OF SOCIOECONOMIC STATUS AND ACCULTURATION

While the figures above provide some sense of how levels of segregation from whites vary by ethnicity, year of entry, and country of origin, in this section I am interested in examining to what extent patterns of segregation are explained by the characteristics of immigrants, and in particular socioeconomic status and acculturation. This analysis provides further insight into how well the spatial assimilation perspective helps us understand immigrant residential patterns. If, for example, higher-income immigrants and those with greater English-language ability are less residentially segregated from whites than lower-income and non-English-speaking immigrants, then this lends strength to the assimilation perspective. The implication of such findings would be that as immigrants and their children move up the socioeconomic ladder and become more acculturated—the latter as represented in this analysis by English-language fluency—they become less residentially segregated from whites.

To examine these issues, I conducted multivariate analyses, which involved looking at the association between metropolitan-level segregation scores of various groups and those groups' characteristics, as well as the characteristics of the metropolitan areas in which they live. Such analyses can tell us, for example, whether higher-income groups are less segregated from whites than lower-income ones, holding other characteristics constant, such as the groups' sizes, the sizes of the metropolitan areas in which they live, and the regions in which they are located. Appendix A provides more details on the methods used.

Table 2 shows results from these multivariate analyses. In the model 1 that focuses on Hispanic-white segregation in 2000, we see that, consistent with results presented in table 1, foreign-born Hispanics are on average more segregated (0.148 points) from native-born non-Hispanic whites (hereafter *whites*) than are native-born Hispanics. In model 2, when many additional group and metropolitan area characteristics are added to the analysis, we see that the effect of nativity becomes statistically insignificant, indicating that the characteristics of the foreign-born explain their higher levels of segregation. That is, foreign-born Hispanics are more segregated from whites mainly because they have lower incomes and less English fluency than native-born Hispanics.[19] Consistent with the spatial assimilation perspective, the coefficients for

TABLE 2. Generalized Linear Regressions with Levels of Dissimilarity of Hispanics, Asians, and Blacks from Native-Born Non-Hispanic Whites, 2000

	Hispanics		Asians		Blacks	
	Model 1	Model 2	Model 1	Model 2	Model 1	Model 2
Intercept	0.378[a]	0.528[a]	0.388[a]	0.569[a]	0.526[a]	0.263[b]
Native-born (omitted)						
Foreign-born	0.148[a]	−0.021	0.043[a]	0.017	0.120[a]	0.083[a]
Percentage speaking English very well/well		−0.436[a]		−0.216[a]		−0.222[b]
Median household income ($1,000)		−0.002[a]		−0.001[b]		−0.005[a]
Percentage owning a home		−0.055		−0.154[a]		0.053
N	524	524	469	469	428	428
−Log likelihood	447.934	663.691	555.415	691.410	301.567	515.924

SOURCE: John Iceland and Melissa Scopilliti (2008), "Immigrant Residential Segregation in U.S. Metropolitan Areas, 1990–2000." *Demography* 45, 1:79–94.

NOTES: The unit of analysis is the segregation score for a particular race and nativity group in a given metropolitan area. Analysis includes metropolitan areas with at least 1,000 members of the group in question. Model 2 also controls for group size; metropolitan size; percentage minority; percentage employed in manufacturing, government, and military; percentage over sixty-five; percentage enrolled in college; percentage of housing built in the past ten years; percentage living in suburbs; and region.

[a] p < 0.01.

[b] p < 0.05.

English fluency and income in model 2 are indeed statistically significant, indicating that in metropolitan areas where a higher proportion of Hispanics speak English well or very well and have higher household incomes, levels of segregation from non-Hispanic whites are lower.

These findings are generally consistent with prior research on related issues. For example, in a pair of studies that focus on the mobility decisions of Hispanics, Scott South, Kyle Crowder, and Erick Chavez found that those with higher levels of education, income, and English-language proficiency were also more likely to move into neighborhoods with more non-Hispanic whites than were lower-socioeconomic-status Hispanics with less English-language proficiency.[20]

The results here are also generally consistent with residential patterns observed in the Washington, D.C., area. For example, the foreign-born population in the city and the inner suburbs have significantly less English-language proficiency (more than 26 percent report speaking English "not well" or "not at all") than those in the outer suburbs (19.5 percent report the same), and particularly those in the far suburbs (14.8 percent). The outer and far suburbs are areas that contain relatively more non-Hispanic white residents. Immigrants in Washington, D.C., and its inner suburbs are also more likely to be poor than those living farther out.[21]

Results from table 2's model 1 for Asians indicate that, again consistent with spatial assimilation, foreign-born Asians are more segregated from whites than native-born Asians. The coefficient for the foreign-born among Asians (0.043) is smaller than the corresponding one for Hispanics (0.148), indicating that the difference in levels of segregation by nativity is smaller among Asians. As with Hispanics, the foreign-born variable becomes statistically insignificant in model 2, again indicating the importance of group characteristics in explaining the nativity differences. Greater English fluency, home-ownership levels, and income among Asians are all associated with lower levels of Asian-white segregation.

Results from table 2's model 1 for blacks indicate that foreign-born blacks are also more segregated from whites than native-born blacks. However, unlike in model 2 for Hispanics and Asians, group (and metropolitan) characteristics do not explain the higher levels of segregation among the foreign-born. This is in part because black immigrants in fact tend to be of higher average socioeconomic status than native-born blacks. In model 2, we see that higher median income is associated with lower levels of black-white segregation. That the nativity coefficient remains significant in model 2 signifies that other characteristics not in the models—it is hard to know what with the data here—play a role in the particularly high levels of segregation between foreign-born blacks and whites.

Figure 12 illustrates the magnitude of the effect of group and metropolitan characteristics on levels of segregation. More specifically, it simulates, based on the results from the multivariate analyses above, levels of segregation from whites among the foreign-born if they had the same levels of income, English-language ability, and all other characteristics as the native-born of their respective ethnic groups.[22] And because average characteristics of the native-born groups are used in all simulations, we see in figure 12 that segregation scores for all native-born groups are essentially the same.

Perhaps the most striking simulation in figure 12 is the difference in the segregation of foreign-born Hispanics in the model with no control variables (0.53) and the one with a full set of control variables (0.36). This illustrates that foreign-born Hispanics in particular are more segregated from whites than native-born Hispanics because they have characteristics associated with higher segregation. Indeed, once we hold all characteristics constant, we see that levels of segregation from whites among native- and foreign-born Asians and Hispanics are all rather similar and moderate in absolute terms, ranging from 0.36 to 0.41. The effect of nativity is less pronounced among Asians in part because foreign-born Asians have relatively high median incomes and home-ownership levels, especially as compared with foreign-born Hispanics.

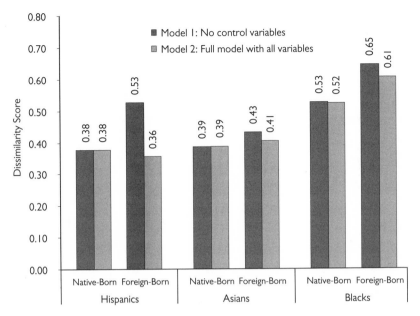

FIGURE 12. Regression simulations: Dissimilarity from native-born non-Hispanic whites by race/ethnicity and nativity, 2000. Source: Analysis of 2000 decennial census data.

Figure 12 also indicates that the average dissimilarity scores are highest among blacks—and foreign-born blacks in particular. When we hold all characteristics constant (model 2), simulations show small declines in the dissimilarity score for foreign-born blacks. This occurs mainly because foreign-born blacks tend to live in metropolitan areas with higher levels of segregation than native-born blacks.[23]

Overall, the results in table 2 and figure 12 provide broad support for the spatial assimilation model: the foreign-born are more segregated from non-Hispanic whites than the native-born, and group characteristics are associated with segregation in expected ways. While these relationships apply to some extent to blacks, the overall high levels of black-white segregation indicate greater overall residential distance between these groups than among Hispanics and whites and Asians and whites.

TABLE 3. Generalized Linear Regressions Indicating the Association between Group and Metropolitan Characteristics with Levels of Dissimilarity of Foreign-Born, by Race and Ethnicity, from Native-Born Non-Hispanic Whites, 2000

	Foreign-Born Hispanics		Foreign-Born Asians		Foreign-Born Blacks		Foreign-Born Whites	
	Model 1	*Model 2*	*Model 1*	*Model 2*	*Model 1*	*Model 2*	*Model 1*	*Model 2*
Intercept	0.604[a]	0.315[a]	0.528[a]	0.503[a]	0.744[a]	0.476[b]	0.460[a]	0.411[a]
Year of entry into the United States								
0–10 years ago (omitted)								
11–20 years ago	−0.024[a]	0.006	−0.031[a]	0.017	−0.031[a]	0.008	−0.029[a]	0.024
21–30 years ago	−0.036[a]	0.011	−0.044[a]	0.031	−0.024	0.030	−0.036[a]	0.026
31+ years ago	−0.097[a]	−0.040	0.013	0.105[a]	−0.003	0.052	−0.176[a]	−0.112[a]
Percentage speaking English very well/well		−0.164[b]		−0.150[b]		−0.105		−0.204[a]
Median household income ($1,000)		−0.001		0.000		−0.002[b]		−0.001[b]
Percentage owning a home		−0.013		−0.116[b]		−0.054		−0.100
N	559	559	535	535	208	208	569	569
−Log likelihood	507.789	678.238	616.042	734.762	236.835	309.989	630.518	776.689

SOURCE: John Iceland and Melissa Scopilliti (2008), "Immigrant Residential Segregation in U.S. Metropolitan Areas, 1990–2000," *Demography* 45, 1:79–94.

NOTES: Analysis includes metropolitan areas with at least 1,000 members of the group in question. Model 2 also controls for group size; metropolitan size; percentage minority; percentage employed in manufacturing, government, and military; percentage over sixty-five; percentage enrolled in college; percentage of housing built in the past ten years; percentage living in suburbs; and region.

[a] p < 0.01.
[b] p < 0.05.

Finally, table 3 shows results of similar multivariate analyses for the foreign-born, only by year of entry. The reference group for these segregation indexes is the same as before: native-born non-Hispanic whites. Patterns among foreign-born non-Hispanic whites and Hispanics are quite similar—the longer the time in the United States, the lower the segregation from native-born non-Hispanic whites (model 1). When we hold other group characteristics constant (model 2), these associations all become statistically insignificant, except among foreign-born non-Hispanic whites who immigrated 31 or more years ago, who show particularly low levels of segregation from native-born non-Hispanic whites. More than immigrants of other ethnic groups, this group of foreign-born whites likely contains many people who immigrated quite a few decades ago.

The year-of-entry coefficients become insignificant in model 2 for Hispanic and white immigrants mainly because longer-term residents have characteristics (e.g., higher English-language fluency or higher incomes) associated with lower levels of segregation. The large differences in segregation by year of entry among white immigrants, and the strong association between group characteristics and segregation, suggests that the spatial assimilation model is particularly good at explaining the residential segregation patterns of foreign-born whites.

Among Asians, results among those who immigrated 11–20 years ago and 21–30 years ago are quite similar to those found among white and Hispanic immigrants. However, we see that those who immigrated 31 years or more ago do not show particularly low levels of segregation, even without holding other characteristics constant (model 1). Moreover, when other characteristics are held constant (model 2), this group actually displays higher levels of segregation than recent arrivals. In other words, levels of segregation would be even higher among these Asian immigrants who have been in the country for decades if they did not have characteristics associated with low levels of segregation—such as high levels of both English-language fluency and home ownership—for reasons that cannot be discerned with the census data used here.

Among black immigrants, only those who arrived 11–20 years ago have lower levels of segregation than the most recent arrivals, and this relationship becomes statistically insignificant when we hold other group and metropolitan area characteristics constant (model 2). However, we do see that higher incomes are associated with lower levels of segregation from whites. These results thus provide mixed support for spatial assimilation. Once again, though, the high overall levels of segregation from whites among all groups of black immigrants rather overshadow the bits of evidence supporting the assimilation paradigm.

CONCLUSIONS

The goal of this chapter has been to examine whether spatial assimilation theory provides a good framework for understanding immigrant residential segregation patterns. I used data from the 1990 and 2000 decennial censuses to calculate dissimilarity indexes for Hispanic, Asian, black, and white immigrants in all U.S. metropolitan areas, using native-born non-Hispanic whites (or *whites*) as the reference group. I then conducted multivariate analyses to determine the extent to which differences in residential segregation can be explained by the characteristics of different groups, such as socioeconomic status and English-language fluency.

In support of spatial assimilation theory, I find that the foreign-born Hispanics, Asians, and blacks are more segregated from whites than the native-born of those groups. In addition, many of the patterns can be explained by the average characteristics of the foreign-born that are generally associated with higher levels of segregation, such as their lower levels of income and English-language fluency. I also find that immigrants who have been in the United States for longer periods of time are generally less segregated than new arrivals, and once again much of this difference can be attributed to the differences in the characteristics of these immigrant groups.

Patterns, however, vary across racial and ethnic groups. Levels of segregation from whites are much higher among black immigrants than among Asian and Hispanic immigrants. In addition, because black immigrants are, on average, of higher socioeconomic status than native-born blacks, such characteristics do little to explain their very high levels of segregation. I also find that non-Hispanic white immigrants are moderately less segregated from native-born whites than Asian and Hispanic immigrants. Moreover, the strong association between white immigrant characteristics and segregation from native-born whites suggests that the spatial assimilation model is particularly good at explaining the residential patterns of white immigrants. In short, these results suggest that the extent and pace of spatial assimilation among immigrants is affected by their race and ethnicity. In absolute terms, levels of segregation from native-born non-Hispanic whites are high for black immigrants, moderate for Hispanic and Asian immigrants, and low to moderate for white immigrants.

It could thus be argued that overall very high levels of segregation among black immigrants in particular provide support for the segmented assimilation perspective. Clearly, black immigrants tend to live in very different neighborhoods than non-Hispanic whites. However, the fact that we see some differences among blacks by nativity, albeit quite small, and some effect of socioeconomic characteristics, mainly income, suggests that support for segmented assimilation (as opposed to spatial assimilation) is not wholly unequivocal.

When examining change between 1990 and 2000, results were often consistent with the spatial assimilation model. Many immigrant cohorts (though not all) experienced small declines in dissimilarity from 1990 to 2000—particularly among Hispanics and non-Hispanic whites. This suggests that the overall observed increase in segregation from whites among the foreign-born between 1990 and 2000 was due to a compositional shift: many of the foreign-born are in fact recent arrivals who are the most likely to live in ethnic enclaves.

The implication of these analyses' support for the spatial assimilation model is that immigrant families will tend to live in more integrated environments the longer they remain in the United States, often as they become more acculturated and gain in socioeconomic status. This is consistent with the view that residential racial and ethnic polarization is not increasing. For example, just as white ethnic groups at one time occupied very different residential niches and thought of themselves (and were thought of by others) as constituting very different groups, over time many of these differences diminished and residential ethnic enclaves weakened.[24]

Two sets of findings provide reason to be cautious about drawing this conclusion too firmly. First, despite some declines in black segregation in the 1990s, blacks and black immigrants continued to be considerably more segregated from whites than other groups. The historical division between blacks and whites in American society, and the continued—albeit declining—discrimination against blacks in the housing market likely still play important roles in shaping residential patterns.[25] Whether the long-run trend of moderate declines in black segregation continues and eventually translates into less polarization and greater integration for black immigrants as well will be an important issue to track in the coming years.

Second, that group characteristics often help explain relatively high levels of segregation among some groups—and among Hispanic immigrants in particular—also has important implications. While it suggests that spatial assimilation processes are at work that could reduce segregation over the longer run, continued high levels of Hispanic immigration, largely consisting of people of low socioeconomic status—precisely the characteristics associated with high levels of dissimilarity—suggest that we should expect increasing levels of segregation for Hispanics in the short and medium term. Over the longer term, we may see declines in Hispanic segregation as second- and third-generation Hispanics experience upward socioeconomic mobility.[26]

CHAPTER 5

Hispanic Segregation and the Multiple Forms of Residential Assimilation in Metropolitan America

The rise in immigration has spurred renewed debate about the trajectory of the American color line. Until recently, this color line has for the most part been all too clearly demarcated. The divide between blacks and whites has been a central one through much of U.S. history. The framers of the Constitution battled over what to do about slavery and the slave trade, and how to count slaves in determining Congressional representation. The legacy of slavery, racism, and discrimination continued to mar race relations through the twentieth century, as exemplified by race riots in places such as Tulsa in 1921, Detroit in 1943, Newark in 1967, and Los Angeles in 1992, among others.

The United States has of course been the site of other kinds of racial and ethnic conflict, including warfare between encroaching white settlers and native American Indian tribes, eventually resulting in the military defeat and marginalization of the latter. In much of the nineteenth and early twentieth centuries, there was broad concern about whether new immigrants could be readily incorporated into society—be they Catholics from Ireland and Germany in the middle of the nineteenth century, or southern and eastern Europeans in the subsequent decades.

As evidenced by the passage of restrictive immigration laws in 1882 and the 1920s, there was also a belief at times that Asians could not and should not be incorporated into American society.

In the course of the twentieth century, distinct ethnic groups hailing from various countries in Europe eventually became to be seen and understood as "white" ethnics.[1] By the latter part of the twentieth century there was also an ideological shift in the United States, such that racial and ethnic discrimination ceased to be tolerated or enshrined in the nation's laws. This view was certainly bitterly opposed by some, but a number of laws were nevertheless enacted to explicitly prohibit discrimination on the basis of race, ethnicity, and national origin. The 1965 Amendments to the Immigration and Nationality Act, for example, eliminated the discriminatory national quota system that favored northern and western Europeans. In the residential sphere, the Fair Housing Act of 1968 made it unlawful to discriminate on the basis of race, color, religion, or national origin in most housing market transactions. This has not prevented discrimination from occurring, but it has affected how business is conducted in the real-estate market.[2] It was as recently as 1967 that the Supreme Court, in *Loving v. Virginia*, struck down state laws barring interracial marriages.

Currently there is continued discussion about the incorporation of the large and growing number of immigrants from Asia, Latin America, and other parts of the globe. Thus far, most analyses indicate that Asians as a whole have high average levels of educational attainment and income, suggesting that Asians are by and large faring well in the American economy. This does not mean that Asians face no obstacles or challenges as a racial minority in the United States; rather, it appears that existing barriers are not so high as to greatly impede socioeconomic achievement of Asians in America.[3] Previous chapters have also shown rather moderate levels of residential segregation between Asians and whites in U.S. metropolitan areas. Further, a relatively high proportion of Asians marry non-Asians, consistent with the notion that Asians are assimilating into U.S. society.[4]

In this era of greater racial and ethnic diversity, some have argued that the traditional black-white divide should more aptly be described as a "white-nonwhite" divide or, alternatively, a "black-nonblack" divide.[5] The existence of a white-nonwhite divide would suggest a context of exclusive white privilege, where all minority groups are disadvantaged in various spheres of American life. In contrast, a black-nonblack divide denotes black exceptionalism, that blacks face unparalleled levels of discrimination and are thus uniquely disadvantaged. Frank Bean and Gillian Stevens, in their 2003 book on the economic and social incorporation of recent immigrants in the United States, conclude after a review of these issues that "what sets the experiences of Latinos and Asians apart from those of African Americans is that the former are not rooted in a historical legacy of slavery and its resultant consequences of legal, systematic, and persistent discrimination and inequality from which the tenacious black-white divide was born. . . . At this time, the unequal pace at which the color line is shifting for these three groups [blacks, Asians, and Latinos] points to the emergence of a black-nonblack divide according to which Latinos and Asians are placed closer to whites than to blacks."[6]

Similarly, Philip Kasinitz and his colleagues assert that while the central rift in American life was traditionally between whites and nonwhites (in the civil rights movement it was widely observed that assimilation had historically been for "whites only"),[7] today there is some evidence that such a rift exists more between blacks and nonblacks. Kasinitz argues that the civil rights movement improved the situation of all minority members (including blacks), and that "the second generation of recent immigrants is well positioned to take advantage of the reforms put in place to remedy past discrimination against African Americans."[8] Indeed, immigrants are generally overrepresented at high-status universities and even among black college students as well.[9]

These are of course not the last words on the location of the color line. Not only is further analysis of these issues needed, but the social and economic climate also continues to change. In this chapter I delve into these issues by examining the residential patterns of Hispanics. Hispanics are of course quite heterogeneous, as the term refers to a group of people from different countries with varied histories and also coming to the United States under different conditions. Cuban refugees migrating to Miami, for example, differ markedly in many respects from Dominicans in New York City in their socioeconomic profile. Some Hispanics never immigrated to the United States per se; they were incorporated with the U.S. annexation of territory in Florida and the American Southwest in the first half of the nineteenth century.

In this analysis I am particularly interested in the roles that race and nativity play in shaping Hispanic residential patterns.[10] While many studies have found that Hispanic-Anglo residential segregation is lower than African American–Anglo segregation, comparisons of Hispanic racial subgroups have been relatively rare. (For the sake of simplicity I often use the term *Anglo* to refer to native-born non-Hispanic whites in this chapter.) This stems in part from the ambiguous nature of racial and ethnic identity among Hispanics. Collecting race information from Hispanics has historically been problematic given the diversity of origins among Hispanics living in the United States and confusion over the distinction between Hispanic ethnicity and race classification in the U.S. context.[11] While the United States has a history of dichotomizing race into white and black, exemplified by the "one drop rule"—where people having any African heritage were considered black—in Latin America race is a multicategory continuum.[12] In addition, many Latin Americans consider themselves to be a mix of Spanish and Indian ancestry, which is a category unto its own (mestizo).

There is even some confusion about the meaning of race and ethnicity among social scientists. The general tendency is to define *race* as a social construction based on physiological—particularly phenotypical—differences and *ethnicity* as a social construction based mainly on cultural differences between groups. But the meanings of these terms have changed over time and sometimes they are also used interchangeably. Some have called for more rigor in disentangling them as empirical phenomena. For example, it has been argued that ethnicity might better be thought of as a more fluid indicator of identity often defined by group members themselves, while race is a more rigid classification scheme where individuals' identities are often assigned by outsiders.[13]

In any case, the various sources of confusion about these categories are reflected in the responses to the race and Hispanic origin questions in U.S. government surveys. "Hispanic" or "Latino" is not treated as a "race" in such surveys; rather, two separate questions are typically asked. In the 2000 census and subsequent U.S. Census Bureau surveys, the first question is, "Is this person Spanish/Hispanic/ Latino?" There is an answer box for "no," and then additional "yes" boxes where people also indicate if they are Mexican, Puerto Rican, or Cuban. There is also a write-in box where respondents can identify other origins. The next question on the census and survey forms asks, "What is this person's race?" There are answer boxes for white, black, American Indian or Alaska Native, and a series of boxes for various Asian groups (e.g., Chinese, Filipino, Japanese, etc.). People can also mark "some other race" and, unlike in previous censuses, respondents are instructed that they can choose more than one race.

Data from the 2000 census indicated that 48 percent of Hispanics reported themselves as "white," 2 percent as "black," and the rest as some other combination of race categories on the census form. Forty-two percent explicitly defined themselves as "some other race," as compared with a mere 0.2 percent of the non-Hispanic population.[14]

It is important to note that the reported race of Hispanics is associated with various other socioeconomic outcomes. For example, the median household income in 2000 of U.S.-born white Hispanics averaged across the metropolitan areas in my analysis, at $38,116, is considerably higher than that of native-born black Hispanics ($29,425) and native-born other-race Hispanics ($33,104).[15] Studies have also tended to show that black Hispanics are more segregated from Anglos than are white and other-race Hispanics.[16] Looking at the role of socioeconomic status in shaping residential patterns, as done in this chapter, is thus particularly important for examining the association between race and Hispanic segregation, because in much of Latin America and the Caribbean, people who are socioeconomically successful may be less likely to identify as black.[17] That is, race may refer to both class attainment and skin color in some circumstances.

It is likewise important to look at the role of country of origin in shaping the residential patterns of Hispanics. Immigrants often depend on preexisting community-based networks—networks rooted in their country of origin—when they migrate. This is particularly true among less educated migrants, who often rely on kin and friends who can provide shelter and other kinds of help.[18] A majority of Hispanics in the United States in 2000 reported being Mexican (58.5 percent), with the next-largest groups being Puerto Rican (9.6 percent) and Cuban (3.5 percent).[19] Cubans are the most likely of the three to self-identify as white (84.4 percent in 2000). Puerto Ricans and Mexicans are fairly evenly split between identifying as white and "some other race" (in the 42 to 47 percent range). Puerto Ricans are more likely to self-identify as black (5.8 percent) than Cubans (3.6 percent) or Mexicans (0.7 percent).[20]

Finally, in order to properly understand the trajectory of the color line in the United States, it is important to consider the extent of Hispanic segregation from different groups, not just from whites. Using non-Hispanic whites as the reference group is the traditional choice in studies on residential segregation. This practice is grounded in the notion that non-Hispanic whites are the dominant group in society—economically, politically, and, in many instances, demographically. It is also rooted in the two-group (black-white) paradigm of race relations that was appropriate through much of the twentieth century.

However, according to the spatial assimilation perspective, as articulated by Richard Alba and Victor Nee, assimilation involves the general attenuation of group differences over time and across generations.[21] That is, assimilation means that various groups are not necessarily becoming just like native-born non-Hispanic whites but that residential patterns are to some extent converging among groups. Thus, in this chapter I examine the extent to which different groups of Hispanics might be exhibiting varying or multiple forms of assimilation with other groups. For example, are native-born Hispanics less segregated from both Anglos and African Americans than foreign-born Hispanics? Do these patterns vary by race and country of origin of Hispanics? In answering these questions I hope to present a more nuanced picture of the different forms of spatial assimilation experienced by Hispanics in America.

The central conclusion of the analysis in this chapter is that Hispanic race groups indeed often experience multiple forms of spatial assimilation. In particular, native-born white, black, and other-race Hispanics are all less segregated from both Anglos and African Americans than the foreign-born of the respective groups. Hispanic-race groups also show particularly low levels of segregation from Hispanics not of their own race, indicating the importance of pan-Hispanic identity that spans self-identified race groups. The one exception to this intra-Hispanic pattern occurs among native-born black Hispanics, who are no less segregated from other Hispanic groups than their foreign-born counterparts. The implication of these findings is that assimilation is reducing the significance of various color lines in metropolitan America, except for the modest distancing observed between black and other Hispanic groups.

SEGREGATION OF HISPANICS BY RACE, NATIVITY, AND COUNTRY OF ORIGIN

Figures 13, 14, and 15 present dissimilarity scores of Hispanics by race and nativity, averaged across U.S. metropolitan areas, from native-born (a) Anglos, (b) African Americans, and (c) Hispanics not of the same race group, respectively.[22] The methodology used is detailed in Appendix A. Figure 13 indicates that native-born Hispanics are less segregated from

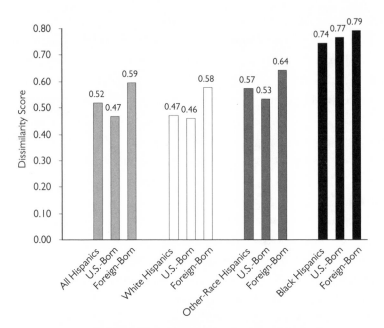

FIGURE 13. Dissimilarity of Hispanics, by race and nativity, from Anglos, 2000. Source: John Iceland and Kyle Anne Nelson (2008), "Hispanic Segregation in Metropolitan America: Exploring the Multiple Forms of Spatial Assimilation," *American Sociological Review* 73, 5:741–65.

Anglos than the foreign-born—consistent with spatial assimilation. However, we also see distinct differences in Hispanic-Anglo segregation by race. White Hispanics are much less segregated from Anglos (0.47) than black Hispanics (0.74). The dissimilarity score for other-race Hispanics (0.57) falls between those of the other two groups, though closer to the white Hispanic score. Again, the general rule of thumb is that dissimilarity scores below 0.3 are considered low, and those above 0.6 are high. Among all groups, the foreign-born are more segregated than the native-born, though the difference is small among black Hispanics.

Figure 14 , where the reference group consists of African Americans, shares some similarities with figure 13. In particular, U.S.-born His-

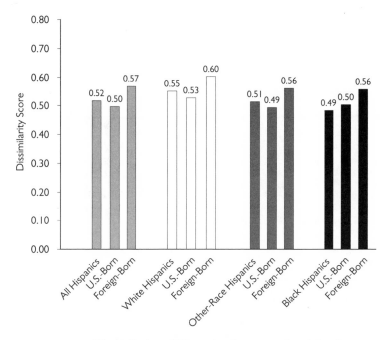

FIGURE 14. Dissimilarity of Hispanics, by race and nativity, from African Americans, 2000. Source: John Iceland and Kyle Anne Nelson (2008), "Hispanic Segregation in Metropolitan America: Exploring the Multiple Forms of Spatial Assimilation," *American Sociological Review* 73, 5:741–65.

panics of all groups are less segregated from African Americans than the foreign-born. This reveals a form of assimilation not commonly discussed in previous studies on the segregation of Hispanics: a generational assimilation of Hispanics not only with Anglos but also with African Americans. These generational patterns conform to research by Camille Charles indicating that, at least in Los Angeles, native-born Hispanics express significantly less aversion to black neighbors than foreign-born Hispanics.[23] In figure 14 the generational differences are also quite similar for all three racial categories of Hispanics, and levels of segregation from African Americans does not substantively differ by race of the Hispanic group.

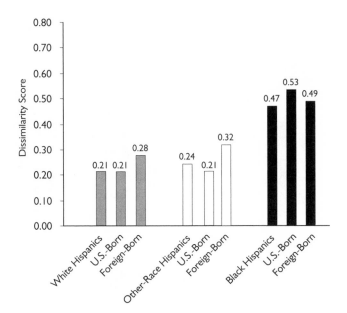

FIGURE 15. Dissimilarity of Hispanics, by race and nativity, from native-born Hispanics not of same race, 2000. Source: John Iceland and Kyle Anne Nelson (2008), "Hispanic Segregation in Metropolitan America: Exploring the Multiple Forms of Spatial Assimilation," *American Sociological Review* 73, 5:741–65.

A comparison of figures 13 and 14 also indicates that white Hispanics are less segregated from Anglos than from African Americans, but black Hispanics are considerably less segregated from African Americans than from Anglos. This finding is consistent with those of other studies that have examined generational differences.[24] Other-race Hispanics are fairly similarly segregated from both African Americans and Anglos.

Figure 15 indicates that levels of white and other-race Hispanic segregation from native-born Hispanics of a different race group are all quite low—in the 0.21 to 0.32 range. For these two groups we once again see a pattern of assimilation—the native-born are less segregated from other Hispanic race groups than the foreign-born. This suggests yet another form of assimilation: a growth in Hispanic neighborhoods less divided by race across generations. This is consistent with other research indicating that pan-ethnic self-identification tends to increase with time in the United States and is more common among U.S.-born children of immigrants than among children who themselves are foreign-born.[25]

Notably, for black Hispanics we see a different pattern. U.S.-born black Hispanics are actually more segregated from other U.S.-born Hispanic race groups than the foreign-born, and levels of segregation are on the whole higher as well. This suggests that black Hispanics are not becoming residentially more similar to U.S.-born Hispanics of different races. Whether this suggests a differential selection of individuals self-identifying as "black" among native-born Hispanics who feel apart from other Hispanics in the second and higher generations, or truly different patterns by nativity and phenotype, we cannot say with the data available here. In any case, we see a markedly different pattern among Hispanics who self-identify as black.

Residential Patterns of Hispanics in Washington, D.C.

Metropolitan Washington, D.C., once again provides a good illustration of Hispanic residential patterns. The overall black-Anglo dissimilarity score in the D.C. metropolitan area, at 0.64 in 2000, was higher than the Hispanic-Anglo one (0.49). The black-Hispanic dissimilarity score, at 0.57, was somewhere in between. As discussed in the previous chapter, non-Hispanic whites are concentrated on the western side of D.C. itself and then widely distributed across the suburbs, though less so in Prince George's County, directly east of the city. In contrast, African Americans are concentrated on the eastern side of D.C. and in Prince George's County, but to some extent in other suburbs as well, such as Charles County, to the south. Reflecting their moderate segregation from both groups, Hispanics are clustered in the north-central part of the city and also in a variety of inner-suburban counties, such as Montgomery County and the northern part of Prince George's. Indeed, Prince George's County is a popular destination for many mobile Hispanic immigrants seeking affordable suburban living.[26]

Census data from 2000 indicate that white and other-race Hispanics in fact reside in many of the same neighborhoods across the Washington metropolitan area, illustrating the low levels of dissimilarity between them (0.25). There are relatively few black Hispanics in metropolitan Washington, as in the nation as a whole. Black Hispanics occupy some of the same inner suburbs as white and other-race Hispanics (black Hispanic dissimilarity from these groups is 0.55 and 0.52, respectively). Nevertheless, as reflected in the moderate to high dissimilarity scores between black Hispanics and other Hispanics, there are relatively more black Hispanics in Prince George's County, to the east of the city, where the native-born African American population is also concentrated. The black Hispanic–African American dissimilarity score, at 0.53, is indeed a bit lower than the dissimilarity scores between African Americans and white Hispanics and between African Americans and other-race Hispanics, at 0.60 and 0.59, respectively. Likewise, white Hispanics are less segregated from Anglos (0.43) than black (0.67) and other-race (0.57) Hispanics.

Residential Patterns of Hispanics by Race and Country of Origin

Table 4 shows the average metropolitan-level segregation scores depicted in figures 13, 14, and 15 and also provides more detailed dissimilarity scores for Mexicans, Cubans, and Puerto Ricans.[27] Because there are fewer than 100,000 foreign-born black Mexicans, black Cubans, or black Puerto Ricans in the United States (the population cutoff used in this study), there is no data to present for these specific groups. Table 4 shows Puerto Ricans as a whole to be slightly more segregated from Anglos (0.60) than Mexicans (0.54) or Cubans (0.54), though Cubans are the most segregated from African Americans.

Indeed, other research also suggests that Cubans in particular are more likely to live in neighborhoods with Anglos than other Hispanic groups. Cubans in Miami, for example, have been both socioeconomically and residentially mobile. As a result, Cuban-Anglo segregation has declined in recent years, while Cuban-black segregation remains high.[28] Puerto Ricans, on the other hand, have historically been more segregated from Anglos than other Hispanic groups, and they continued to be so in 2000. However, some studies have documented recent declines in Puerto Rican–Anglo segregation, which is all the more apparent in newer metropolitan areas with growing Puerto Rican communities where socioeconomic inequality is less pervasive, such as Orlando, Florida.[29]

Table 4 also shows that Mexicans are a little more segregated from Anglos than from African Americans. This represents a small reversal from 1990, when Mexicans were slightly more segregated from African Americans than from Anglos, according to data from other studies.[30] Why this occurred is not clear. It could reflect that a large proportion of Mexicans are relatively low-skill immigrants who can more afford to live in lower-income African American areas than in Anglo areas. The issue is discussed in more detail in the following section.

Despite some general differences in levels of segregation across the three country-of-origin groups, we see assimilation patterns among the groups that mirror the overall findings for Hispanics as a whole. For example, providing support for the spatial assimilation model, foreign-born Mexicans, Cubans, and Puerto Ricans who are white are more segregated from Anglos than the native-born of those respective groups. Although the decennial census does not allow differentiating across generations among the native-born, research by Susan Brown on the residential patterns of Mexicans in the Los Angeles metropolitan area suggests that spatial integration becomes particularly evident among third-generation Mexicans, and less so before.[31]

In table 4, however, we see one important assimilation-related pattern by country of origin that differs from the overall Hispanic one. Contrary to the patterns among all of the white Hispanics and white

TABLE 4. Mean Dissimilarity Scores for Hispanics by Nativity, Race, and Place of Birth, 2000

	Anglos		African Americans		U.S.-Born Hispanics Not of Same Race Group	
	Number of Metropolitan Areas	Dissimilarity	Number of Metropolitan Areas	Dissimilarity	Number of Metropolitan Areas	Dissimilarity
All Hispanics	**302**	**0.519**	**280**	**0.519**	—	—
U.S.-born	288	0.469	268	0.496	—	—
Foreign-born	242	0.595	231	0.568	—	—
White Hispanics	273	0.471	254	0.550	242	0.213
U.S.-born	251	0.422	235	0.529	236	0.215
Foreign-born	204	0.558	198	0.603	199	0.276
Other-race Hispanics	263	0.575	245	0.515	250	0.241
U.S.-born	237	0.533	220	0.494	234	0.208
Foreign-born	217	0.642	208	0.561	214	0.318
Black Hispanics	88	0.744	88	0.486	88	0.471
U.S.-born	68	0.766	68	0.503	68	0.533
Foreign-born	31	0.792	31	0.559	31	0.489

Mexico	**267**	**0.542**	**247**	**0.523**	—	—
U.S.-born	244	0.483	226	0.500	—	—
Foreign-born	200	0.639	189	0.580	—	—
White	227	0.512	214	0.540	220	0.203
U.S.-born	201	0.453	190	0.526	200	0.206
Foreign-born	151	0.632	145	0.600	150	0.287
Other race	225	0.583	211	0.526	220	0.260
U.S.-born	186	0.535	175	0.501	186	0.218
Foreign-born	170	0.660	162	0.581	168	0.347
Black	29	0.824	29	0.676	29	0.684
U.S.-born	22	0.838	22	0.676	22	0.720
Foreign-born	—	—	—	—	—	—

(continued)

TABLE 4. (continued)

| | REFERENCE GROUP | | | | | |
| | Anglos | | African Americans | | U.S.-Born Hispanics Not of Same Race Group | |
	Number of Metropolitan Areas	Dissimilarity	Number of Metropolitan Areas	Dissimilarity	Number of Metropolitan Areas	Dissimilarity
HISPANIC-ORIGIN SUBGROUPS						
Cuba	**67**	**0.538**	**67**	**0.775**	—	—
U.S.-born	44	0.518	44	0.770	—	—
Foreign-born	43	0.575	43	0.800	—	—
White	57	0.538	57	0.802	57	0.480
U.S.-born	32	0.508	32	0.804	32	0.517
Foreign-born	35	0.572	35	0.819	35	0.485
Other race	23	0.690	23	0.783	23	0.521
U.S.-born	—	—	—	—	—	—
Foreign-born	—	—	—	—	—	—
Black	—	—	—	—	—	—
U.S.-born	—	—	—	—	—	—
Foreign-born	—	—	—	—	—	—

Puerto Rico	**145**	**0.602**	**145**	**0.550**	—	—
U.S.-born	123	0.593	123	0.553	—	—
Foreign-born	98	0.658	98	0.583	—	—
White	113	0.554	113	0.598	112	0.332
U.S.-born	93	0.551	93	0.617	93	0.380
Foreign-born	69	0.614	69	0.617	69	0.338
Other race	107	0.698	107	0.573	107	0.391
U.S.-born	87	0.692	87	0.579	87	0.397
Foreign-born	61	0.751	61	0.607	61	0.433
Black	34	0.823	34	0.558	34	0.544
U.S.-born	26	0.839	26	0.568	26	0.578
Foreign-born	—	—	—	—	—	—

SOURCE: John Iceland and Kyle Anne Nelson (2008), "Hispanic Segregation in Metropolitan America: Exploring the Multiple Forms of Spatial Assimilation," *American Sociological Review* 73, 5:741–65.

NOTE: Analysis includes only those metropolitan areas with at least 1,000 weighted cases in the relevant population groups. Scores are weighted by the size of the population group of interest. As Puerto Ricans are U.S. citizens at birth, the foreign-born category for this group refers to those born in Puerto Rico.

Mexicans in particular, white Cubans and Puerto Ricans show a strong pattern of generational assimilation with Anglos but not with Hispanics not of the same race. In other words, this suggests that, over generations, Cubans and Puerto Ricans who self-identify as white are becoming residentially more similar to Anglos, but not to other nonwhite Hispanics. In contrast, white and other-race Mexicans are increasingly likely to live with Hispanics of other races across generations, suggesting a greater importance of Hispanic origin than race among Mexicans.

THE ROLE OF SOCIOECONOMIC STATUS AND ACCULTURATION

While the table and figures above provide some sense of how Hispanic segregation varies by race, nativity, and country of origin, in this section I am interested in examining to what extent these patterns are explained by the characteristics of the different groups, mainly socioeconomic status and English-language fluency. As in chapter 4, to examine these issues I conducted multivariate analyses, which involved looking at the association between metropolitan-level segregation scores of various groups and those groups' characteristics, as well as the characteristics of the metropolitan areas in which they live. Appendix A provides more details on the methods used.

These results are reported in tables 5, 6, and 7. Table 5 focuses on the segregation of Hispanics from Anglos in particular. Before taking into account group and metropolitan characteristics (models 1, 3, and 5), we again see that native-born white, black, and other-race Hispanics are less segregated from Anglos than the foreign-born of the respective groups. For example, U.S.-born white Hispanics have segregation scores that are, on average, 0.171 points lower than those among foreign-born white Hispanics. Note that the nativity difference is largest for white Hispanics and smallest for black Hispanics, suggesting greater assimilation with Anglos among the former group than among the latter group.

TABLE 5. Generalized Linear Regressions with Levels of Dissimilarity of Hispanics, by Race, from Anglos, 2000

	White Hispanics		Black Hispanics		Other-Race Hispanics	
	Model 1	Model 2	Model 3	Model 4	Model 5	Model 6
Intercept	0.531[a]	0.470[a]	0.803[a]	0.768[a]	0.575[a]	0.351[a]
Nativity						
Native-born	–0.171[a]	–0.096[a]	–0.054[a]	–0.068[b]	–0.111[a]	0.003
Foreign-born (omitted)						
Other group-specific characteristics						
Hispanic/Anglo ratio of median household income		–0.097[b]		–0.111[a]		–0.129[a]
Percentage speaking English very well/well		–0.135[b]		0.020		–0.293[a]
Percentage owning a home		–0.127[a]		–0.027		–0.026
Country of origin						
Mexico (omitted)						
Cuba		–0.234[a]		–0.329[a]		–0.266
Puerto Rico		0.022		–0.144[a]		0.076
All other origins		–0.047		–0.104[a]		–0.052
DF	453	434	97	78	452	433
–Log likelihood	450.310	610.827	109.593	174.204	372.943	580.563

SOURCE: John Iceland and Kyle Anne Nelson (2008), "Hispanic Segregation in Metropolitan America: Exploring the Multiple Forms of Spatial Assimilation," *American Sociological Review* 73, 5:741–65.

NOTES: The unit of analysis is the segregation score for a particular group in a given metropolitan area. Analysis includes metropolitan areas with at least 1,000 members of the group in question. Models 2, 4, and 6 also control for group size; metropolitan size; percentage minority; percentage employed in manufacturing, government, and military; percentage over sixty-five; percentage enrolled in college; percentage of housing built in the past ten years; percentage living in suburbs; and region.

[a] $p < 0.01$.
[b] $p < 0.05$.

Taking group characteristics into account (in models 2, 4, and 6) narrows the difference between the native-born and foreign-born of each race group. This indicates that nativity differences are explained in part by differences in group characteristics. That is, native-born white Hispanics, for example, are less segregated from Anglos than foreign-born white Hispanics because they have on average higher incomes.[32] Indeed, we see that for all groups, higher incomes (as measured relative to Anglo incomes) are associated with lower levels of segregation from Anglos. Among white and other-race Hispanics, English fluency is also associated with lower segregation from Anglos. We further see that, in metropolitan areas with a higher proportion of Cubans, dissimilarity scores vis-à-vis Anglos are lower for white and black Hispanics.

These findings are again broadly consistent with the findings from a pair of analyses by Scott South, Kyle Crowder, and Erick Chavez on the mobility patterns of Hispanic immigrants. They reported that high-socioeconomic-status Hispanics and those with greater English-language use are indeed more likely to move into neighborhoods with more non-Hispanic whites than low-socioeconomic-status Hispanics with less English-language fluency.[33]

Table 6 shows analogous results but with African Americans as the reference group in the segregation calculations. As in table 5, we see that, before taking into account differences in group and metropolitan area characteristics, the native-born are all less segregated from African Americans than the foreign-born of the respective Hispanic groups (models 1, 3, and 5). The differences in segregation by nativity is this time largest among black Hispanics (−0.106) and substantively similar for white (−0.043) and other-race (−0.050) Hispanics.

Taking group and metropolitan characteristics into account does not have a uniform effect on all Hispanic groups, and the effects of the group characteristics themselves tend to be statistically insignificant, suggesting that they are not all that useful in helping us understand Hispanic–African American segregation patterns in U.S. metropolitan areas.[34] The main exception is that among white Hispanics, higher

TABLE 6. Generalized Linear Regressions with Levels of Dissimilarity of Hispanics, by Race, from African Americans, 2000

	White Hispanics		Black Hispanics		Other-Race Hispanics	
	Model 1	Model 2	Model 3	Model 4	Model 5	Model 6
Intercept	0.539[a]	−0.178	0.659[a]	0.319	0.529[a]	−0.048
Nativity						
Native-born	−0.043[a]	−0.018	−0.106[a]	−0.123[a]	−0.050[a]	−0.046
Foreign-born (omitted)						
Other group-specific characteristics						
Hispanic/African American ratio of median household income		0.071[a]		0.048		0.007
Percentage speaking English very well/well		−0.081		−0.012		−0.001
Percentage owning a home		−0.008		−0.058		−0.079
Country of origin						
Mexico (omitted)						
Cuba		0.118		0.111		0.108
Puerto Rico		0.064		−0.086		0.062
All other origins		0.095		−0.172[b]		−0.017
DF	453	434	97	78	452	433
−Log likelihood	283.267	417.770	93.262	135.586	285.870	386.751

SOURCE: John Iceland and Kyle Anne Nelson (2008), "Hispanic Segregation in Metropolitan America: Exploring the Multiple Forms of Spatial Assimilation," *American Sociological Review* 73, 5:741–65.

NOTES: The unit of analysis is the segregation score for a particular group in a given metropolitan area. Analysis includes metropolitan areas with at least 1,000 members of the group in question. Models 2, 4, and 6 also control for group size; metropolitan size; percentage minority; percentage employed in manufacturing, government, and military; percentage over sixty-five; percentage enrolled in college; percentage of housing built in the past ten years; percentage living in suburbs; and region.

[a] p < 0.01.
[b] p < 0.05.

incomes relative to those of African Americans are associated with higher segregation from African Americans (this coefficient is also positive, but statistically insignificant, for black and other-race Hispanics). Conversely, in metropolitan areas where Hispanics have relatively low incomes, Hispanics may be more likely to share neighborhoods with African Americans.

These findings on the role of income in the residential decisions of Hispanics receive some anecdotal support in the Washington, D.C., metropolitan area. A 2007 *Washington Post* article described how the housing boom of the early 2000s made many of the traditional, high-amenity suburban areas, such as in Montgomery and Prince William counties (which have a significant representation of whites), unaffordable for many Hispanics. Thus, many working-class Hispanics were buying homes in the largely low-income African American neighborhoods in southeast Washington.[35] Essentially, rising demand spurred by rapid population growth led Hispanics to consider living in a broader range of neighborhoods in the metropolitan area. This process has likely also occurred in a number of metropolitan areas across the country, such as Chicago and Los Angeles, where many low-income neighborhoods that had been African American for decades are now largely mixed or even majority Latino.[36]

Finally, table 7 shows results with native-born Hispanics not of the same race as the reference group in the segregation calculations.[37] We see here that, as indicated earlier, foreign-born white Hispanics and other-race Hispanics are more segregated from native-born Hispanics of a different race than the native-born of the respective groups, suggesting a process of spatial assimilation with Hispanics of other races across generations. However, there is no significant nativity difference for black Hispanics.

Among white Hispanics, greater relative income and English-language ability are both associated with greater segregation from non-white Hispanics. However, greater home ownership is associated with lower levels of segregation from other Hispanics. Why we see

TABLE 7. Generalized Linear Regressions with Levels of Dissimilarity of Hispanics, by Race, from Native-Born Hispanics Not of Same Race, 2000

	White Hispanics		Black Hispanics		Other-Race Hispanics	
	Model 1	Model 2	Model 3	Model 4	Model 5	Model 6
Intercept	0.352[a]	−0.272[b]	0.598[a]	0.560[b]	0.388[a]	0.007
Nativity						
Native-born	−0.037[a]	−0.138[a]	0.001	−0.061	−0.088[a]	−0.122[a]
Foreign-born (omitted)						
Other group-specific characteristics						
Hispanic/native-born Hispanics not of same race ratio of median household income		0.122[a]		−0.035		0.049
Percentage speaking English very well/well		0.290[a]		0.157		0.100
Percentage owning a home		−0.228[a]		−0.007		−0.304[a]
Country of origin						
Mexico (omitted)						
Cuba		0.174[a]		−0.114		−0.026
Puerto Rico		−0.106		−0.307[a]		0.001
All other origins		0.098		−0.223[a]		−0.020
DF	453	434	97	78	452	433
−Log likelihood	295.670	467.930	76.395	138.223	334.559	498.475

SOURCE: John Iceland and Kyle Anne Nelson (2008), "Hispanic Segregation in Metropolitan America: Exploring the Multiple Forms of Spatial Assimilation," *American Sociological Review* 73, 5:741–65.

NOTES: The unit of analysis is the segregation score for a particular group in a given metropolitan area. Analysis includes metropolitan areas with at least 1,000 members of the group in question. Models 2, 4, and 6 also control for group size; metropolitan size; percentage minority; percentage employed in manufacturing, government, and military; percentage over sixty-five; percentage enrolled in college; percentage of housing built in the past ten years; percentage living in suburbs; and region.

[a] p < 0.01.
[b] p < 0.05.

different relationships between segregation and these two indicators of socioeconomic status is not entirely clear. Perhaps, consistent with evidence from other studies, it is a matter of Hispanic home seekers being more likely to be steered to Hispanic neighborhoods, regardless of their income.[38]

CONCLUSIONS

A notable finding of this chapter is that we see a pattern of assimilation of Hispanics not only with Anglos but also with African Americans. Moreover, Hispanic race groups also show particularly low levels of segregation from native-born Hispanics not of their own race, indicating the general salience of pan-Hispanic identity that crosses racial lines.

These findings are generally consistent with research by Michael White, Ann Kim, and Jennifer Glick that describes how, in diverse societies, it has become increasingly important to recognize that individuals can become integrated with multiple groups.[39] In other words, "assimilation" should not be simply thought of as an indicator of the extent to which a group is becoming just like non-Hispanic whites. Rather, we should consider it more generally as a reduction in group differences, and in fact particular groups can experience a reduction in differences from a number of other groups.

Take the traditional notion of the assimilation process, in which immigrants are initially drawn to an ethnic enclave. The analysis here suggests that over time and across generations some group members will live in neighborhoods with a greater number of whites, while others will live in a neighborhood with more African Americans. Decisions to move are based in part on a whole series of calculations concerning the amenities one can afford in alternative locations, and naturally these calculations tip in different directions for different households.

This is not to say that race plays little role in shaping residential patterns. The findings here, for example, indicate that white Hispanics are in general less segregated from Anglos than from African Americans, and black Hispanics are considerably less segregated from African Americans than from Anglos. As other research suggests, it is possible that discrimination in the housing market, such as the steering of different groups by real-estate agents to certain neighborhoods, and perhaps hostility people feel in different locations in a metropolitan area still play a role in shaping residential patterns.[40] For example, black Hispanics may feel more comfortable living in neighborhoods with African Americans than with whites and/or may be steered by real-estate agents to predominately black neighborhoods.

We also see a couple of exceptions to the general patterns of generational assimilation. U.S.-born black Hispanics are not less segregated from other Hispanic groups than the foreign-born. This suggests that black Hispanics are not becoming residentially more similar to Hispanics of different races. Contrary to the patterns among all of the white Hispanics and white Mexicans in particular, we also find that white Cubans and white Puerto Ricans show a strong pattern of assimilation with Anglos but not with Hispanics of other races.

What, then, can be made of the paradoxical finding that Hispanic groups tend to display lower levels of segregation from both Anglos and African Americans while at the same time there is a modest distancing between some Hispanic race groups across generations? I venture that there are two processes at work. First, we have conventional (if rather modest) assimilation between Hispanics and preexisting native-born groups—both African Americans and Anglos. At the same time, as Denton and Massey have argued, immigrants become acclimated to the local—American—racial hierarchy, which results, in some cases, in the distancing between some Hispanic race groups.[41] That is not to say that racism is absent in the countries of origin, but rather that racial distinctions are more clearly delineated in the United States.

Second, it is also important to acknowledge that racial identity can itself be shaped by one's circumstances, and this could play a role in the results. That is, it is possible that living in a black neighborhood or not achieving economic success can affect one's identification, and not just vice versa. For example, sociologist Mary Waters describes how second-generation black immigrants who are middle class are more likely than lower-income immigrants to emphasize their ethnic identity—their country of origin—than a "black" racial American identity.[42] She did not study how these different groups would actually respond to the race question on a government survey, per se, but it seems possible that some who adopt an ethnic identity might be more likely to respond as "some other race" than "black." On the other hand, Scott South and his colleagues, in a study of spatial assimilation of U.S. Latinos, found that skin color, as judged by interviewers, does play a role in individuals' mobility patterns. In particular, they found that, holding a number of other factors constant, darker-skinned Puerto Ricans and Cubans were less likely to move into Anglo neighborhoods than lighter-skinned ones, suggesting that it is not wholly differences in self-identity that explain residential patterns.[43]

How these processes will play out over the long run certainly remains in question. I further venture, however, that the multiple forms of assimilation we find will largely reduce the significance of various color lines in metropolitan America. That is, immigrant families will tend to live in more integrated environments the longer they remain in the United States. However, echoing chapter 4, there is reason to be cautious about too firmly drawing this conclusion. Despite some declines in black segregation from other groups in the 1990s, African Americans and black Hispanics continued to be highly segregated from Anglos and other Hispanics. It is fair to say that the divergent residential patterns observed among black Hispanics are in fact more consistent with the predictions of segmented assimilation (described in chapter 2) than with those of spatial assimilation. Whether the long-run trend of moderate declines in African American segregation continues and eventually translates into greater integration for black Hispanics as well will be an important issue to track in the coming years. It is possible that we could see a hardening of the division between blacks, including black Hispanics, and other groups.

This would also be consistent with research suggesting that black immigrants tend to develop a shared racial group identity with African Americans over time, though the meaning attached to black identity often varies.[44] For example, while West Indian immigrants often share a common identity with African Americans, they still see themselves as distinct in many ways and often attempt to maintain this distinctiveness by avoiding the negative stereotypes ascribed to the African American population. However, many end up identifying as black because the broader population defines and treats them in that way.[45]

CHAPTER 6

Racial and Ethnic Diversity
and Residential Segregation

The implications of the increasing racial and ethnic diversity wrought by immigration for patterns of segregation, neighborhood stability, and group conflict are not well understood. Indeed, communities across the United States are grappling with such population change. The *Kansas City Star*, for example, described how a local nonprofit recently launched a pilot diversity program in Platte and Clay counties in Missouri. This program hopes to make newcomers feel more welcome by helping community members engage in conversations about race, ethnicity, and cultural identity. The impetus for the program was the heavy inflow of immigrants in recent years (the population of both counties increased by about 12.5 percent from 2000 to 2006). "It's real all of a sudden," the organization's director, James Rice, told the *Star*. He called it "diversity times three," with an influx of immigrants from places such as Sudan and Bosnia, as well as growing Hispanic and black populations. "It's actually quite wonderful," said Rice.[1]

One might think that Rice, as a director of a diversity program, has reason to appreciate growing diversity. Diversity, however, can also raise a number of challenges. In diverse areas there is often competition for control of local governance and resources. To take another example, in 2007 the *Washington Post* ran a story about how in Fairfax County,

Virginia, Vellie Dietrich Hall kicked off her campaign for a seat on the Fairfax County Board of Supervisors (as a Republican) by asserting that there was not enough diversity on the board.[2] She herself was born in the Philippines and had come to the United States twenty-six years before. Her campaign finance chair was from India, and her two political directors were Korean. The *Post* noted that in Fairfax County, with a population that was 60 percent white, 13 percent Hispanic, 9 percent black, and 16 percent Asian in 2005 (as well 27 percent foreign-born),[3] the board had nine white members and one African American. Hall said that more had to be done to address the challenges of a rapidly urbanizing community, including aging neighborhoods, growth, and crime: "The Board of Supervisors needs a face there that represents the diversity of our community. . . . I want to make sure that these new citizens know that the government exists for them. I can empathize more with what they're going through. I've been there. That is my advantage."[4]

Changes in Gainesville, Georgia, provide a third view of diversity and neighborhood change. Another *Post* story described widespread unease with the high levels of undocumented immigration from Mexico to the area, where a large number of immigrants work in local poultry plants. The story related that an older couple, Uraina and Billy Ray Smith, sold their home in a local subdivision because it was "taken over" by Mexicans who, they said, parked on the grass, jumped into the communal pool in their jeans shorts, and crammed multiple families into the same house. "It used to be a real nice area. Now it's a slum," said Smith. Yet the story also described a restaurant owner in the area who was less concerned with the arrival of illegal immigrants than by the local reaction to them: "Most of [the Mexicans] don't want to come here. They just need to eat. I think we're all God's children, created in his image. . . . And I would hope hearts don't grow to a point where they are so hardened about another human being."[5]

These are but a few examples of how diversity is affecting communities. Indeed, globalization and the increase in immigration worldwide have brought this issue to the fore in many countries. To understand these sets of issues, this chapter addresses the following specific questions: Is diversity serving to increase or reduce racial and ethnic segregation in the United States? How is diversity affecting the residential patterns of native-born whites and blacks? How stable are diverse neighborhoods? What is the quality of group relations in diverse areas? What are the residential patterns of mixed-race individuals, who in some sense are themselves a product of diversity?

PATTERNS OF SEGREGATION
IN THE MULTIETHNIC CONTEXT

The growth of diversity in the United States has naturally led to the rise of many multiethnic metropolitan areas. Studies of the 1970s and 1980s generally showed that black segregation from whites was somewhat lower in such areas.[6] The question arose as to why segregation patterns in multiethnic areas should differ. William Frey and Reynolds Farley hypothesized that the presence of multiple minority groups in general may moderate the traditional stark black-white divide in U.S. communities. Hispanics and Asians may essentially serve as "buffer" groups between initially white and black neighborhoods, resulting in less segregation between blacks and whites.[7]

Here I examine this link between metropolitan diversity and levels of residential segregation in more detail. As in the previous chapter, I do not simply use non-Hispanic whites as the reference group. Rather, I use an index that measures the joint distribution of various racial and ethnic groups: the multigroup information theory index, also known as the multigroup version of the entropy index, or Theil's H. The information theory index is a measure of evenness—the extent to which groups are evenly distributed across neighborhoods.[8] In the course of calculating the information theory index, one also calculates entropy, or diversity, scores, where the higher the number, the more diverse an area. This is not a segregation measure, per se, because it does not measure the distribution of groups across a metropolitan area. A met-

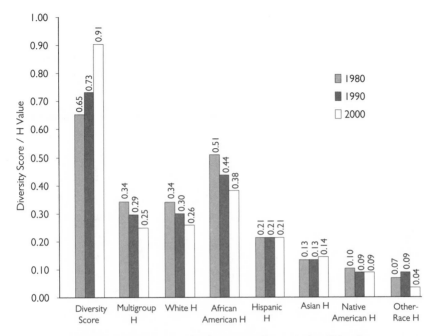

FIGURE 16. Diversity scores and information theory index (H) values, 1980–2000. Source: John Iceland (2004), "Beyond Black and White: Residential Segregation in Multiethnic America," *Social Science Research* 33, 2 (June): 248–71. Note: Higher diversity values indicate greater diversity; higher H values indicate greater segregation. Bars showing equal values can appear slightly different due to rounding.

ropolitan area, for example, can be very diverse if all minority groups are present, but also very highly segregated if all groups live exclusively in their own neighborhoods. Appendix A contains additional information on the measures and methods used here.[9]

Figure 16 shows average diversity scores and H index (segregation) values for U.S. metropolitan areas from 1980 to 2000.[10] We see, as expected, that diversity in U.S. metropolitan areas increased substantially over the period (by 0.26 points, or 40 percent). Over the same period, multigroup segregation declined substantially (by 0.09 points, or 26 percent). Looking at the segregation indexes of the component groups indicates that segregation was greatest for African Americans, followed by that for whites. That is, when looking at the segregation of people of each group vis-à-vis the rest of the population, segregation was high for these two groups. Yet both white and African-American segregation decreased over the period, quite considerably among the latter group. Both of these groups were therefore significantly more evenly distributed across neighborhoods in metropolitan areas in 2000 than in 1980.

The story for Hispanics and Asians differed. Consistent with the figures shown in chapter 3 that were based on the dissimilarity index (also a measure of evenness), Hispanic and Asian segregation remained about the same over the period, though Asian segregation increased slightly. Segregation between American Indians and Alaska Natives and those of other races was less than for other groups and decreased slightly from 1980 to 2000. It should be noted that trends for the "other" race and the American Indian groups should be viewed with caution, given more variability in the definition of the "other" group and changing patterns of self-identification of American Indians over the 1980 to 2000 period.[11]

Overall, these figures indicate that declines in multigroup segregation between 1980 and 2000 were primarily due to declines in the segregation of whites and African Americans from all other groups. These trends raise the question of whether the declines in multigroup segregation were indeed propelled by increasing diversity, or perhaps by other factors altogether.

Multivariate Analysis

To determine whether metropolitan areas that experienced declines in segregation are in fact those that also experienced increases in diversity, I first looked at the link between these two specific variables (i.e., the metropolitan area segregation index and diversity score). Then I replaced the diversity term with what amounts to its component parts— variables representing the change in the percentage of each of the six mutually exclusive groups (white, black, Hispanic, Asian, American Indian, and other) in the metropolitan area. The white category served as the reference, or omitted, category in the analysis. This permits a more detailed examination of whether changes in the representation of particular groups are driving the diversity-segregation relationship. See appendix A for more detail about methods used.

Results from model 1 in table 8 indicate that diversity had a positive relationship with segregation—that is, metropolitan areas that experienced the most rapid increases in diversity tended to experience increases in segregation. The coefficient indicates that an increase in the diversity score of 0.25 points (the average increase between 1980 and 2000) would be associated with an increase in the information theory index of .027.[12] This represents an 8.1 percent increase in segregation. An implication of this finding is that in the absence of rapid growth in diversity, the multigroup entropy index would have fallen by even more than we actually observed in the 1980 to 2000 period.

When diversity is broken down into the component racial and ethnic groups in model 2, results show that increases in the Hispanic and Asian (and "other") populations explain the diversity-segregation relationship. (The coefficients for the "other" and American Indian groups should be viewed with caution, because of the variability in the definition of these groups over the 1980 to 2000 period, as noted above.) In other words, metropolitan areas with less rapid growth in their Hispanic and Asian populations had larger declines in multigroup segregation over the period. This leaves open the question of whether the growth of these groups is mainly affecting Asian and Hispanic segregation in particular, such as through the growth of ethnic enclaves, or if the effect is broader. To address this issue, and also to find out whether diversity more generally has a similar effect on all groups, models 3 through 10 examine the effect of these variables on the segregation of non-Hispanic whites, African Americans, Hispanics, and Asians.

Results from model 3 indicate that growing diversity had a positive association with changes in non-Hispanic white segregation (i.e.,

TABLE 8. Fixed-Effects Regression Results for Changes in Segregation, 1980–2000

	Multigroup H		Non-Hispanic White H		African American H		Hispanic H		Asian H	
	Model 1	Model 2	Model 3	Model 4	Model 5	Model 6	Model 7	Model 8	Model 9	Model 10
Diversity	0.108[a]		0.152[a]		0.132[a]		0.180[a]		0.079[a]	
Racial/ethnic composition										
Change in percentage of population										
White (omitted)										
Black		0.179		0.319		0.246		−0.057		0.099
Hispanic		0.175[b]		0.248[a]		−0.453[a]		0.137[b]		−0.044
Asian		0.513[a]		0.519[a]		−0.172		0.039		0.851[a]
American Indian		0.420		0.152		−1.250		−0.830[b]		0.676
Other		0.535[a]		0.689[a]		0.160		0.182		0.078
N	650	650	650	650	650	650	650	650	650	650
−Log likelihood	1,261.55	1,269.68	1,201.17	1,207.67	1,188.55	1,207.25	1,432.23	1,395.08	1,380.94	1,403.69

SOURCE: John Iceland (2004), "Beyond Black and White: Residential Segregation in Multiethnic America," *Social Science Research* 33, 2 (June): 248–71.

NOTES: The dependent variable is the change in the information theory index (H) in a metropolitan area in a given decade. Models also control for decade of change.

[a] p < 0.01.
[b] p < 0.05.

more diversity was associated with greater white segregation). Model 4, which looks at the effect of the growth of component racial and ethnic groups, indicates that decreases in white segregation were less likely in places with increasing populations of Hispanics, Asians, and "others." Thus, for whites, it appears that greater diversity was associated with increasing segregation.

Model 5, which shows the results for African Americans, tells a different story. Increasing diversity was associated with declining African American segregation from other groups. Model 6 indicates that the growth in the Hispanic population in particular was associated with declining black segregation. Models 7 and 9, which show the results for Hispanics and Asians, indicate that growing diversity had a positive association with both Hispanic and Asian segregation. The results in models 8 and 10 indicate that the growth in the Hispanic and Asian populations in particular was associated with increases in Hispanic and Asian segregation, respectively.

In summary, results from these analyses indicate that general declines in multigroup segregation from 1980 to 2000 occurred *despite* increasing diversity. This was particularly true for white, Hispanic, and Asian segregation from other groups. Notably, however, increasing diversity was associated with declining segregation of African Americans from others. This is consistent with the notion that other groups—and Hispanics in particular—may serve as "buffer" groups between initially white and black neighborhoods, resulting in less segregation between blacks and others.[13]

Also consistent with these findings for African Americans is research indicating that black-white segregation is low and declining in metropolitan areas in the "new" South and West, which also have growing Hispanic and Asian populations. These metropolitan areas also tend to have relatively small, but growing, African American populations without entrenched ghettos of the magnitude seen in older metropolitan areas in the Northeast and Midwest. As Frey and Farley assert: "The history of racial antagonism between blacks and whites in these multiethnic metropolitan areas is neither as long nor as intense as those in many Northeastern, Midwestern, and Southern metros that are classified as 'mostly black-white.' Moreover, the blacks in multiethnic metropolitan areas include larger numbers of 'second wave' [African American] migrants who relocated from northern metropolitan locations, following mainstream job market paths and often possessing more education than members of the 'first wave' [African American migrants who left the South for industrial centers in the early and middle decades of the twentieth century]."[14]

These multiethnic metropolitan areas include places such as Houston, Miami, and Las Vegas—all of which experienced declines in the segregation of blacks from other groups in the 1980s (the period of Frey and Farley's study).[15] Mary Fischer and Marta Tienda also note that metropolitan areas that are serving as "new Hispanic destinations" are among those that experienced substantial decreases in black segregation from other groups, again suggesting that Hispanic dispersal may indeed be softening established color lines.[16]

Among Hispanics and Asians, the positive association between diversity and segregation in the multivariate analysis was explained mainly by the increases in the Hispanic and Asian populations, respectively. This suggests that this group-specific population growth may be buttressing Hispanic and Asian ethnic enclaves. As also suggested by the analysis in chapter 4, it is quite likely that continued high levels of immigration may be increasing segregation, at least in the short run, even as the native-born of those groups are moving to more integrated communities.

The positive association between diversity and white segregation (more diversity is associated with greater white segregation from other groups) suggests a couple of alternative explanations. On the one hand, these findings are consistent with the hypothesis that whites avoid diverse areas. On the other hand, it could also be that forces producing the positive association between Asian and Hispanic segregation from others—the inflow of many recent immigrants who tend to display higher levels of segregation—are also serving to, at least in the short run, produce greater white segregation from others in these diverse areas. After all, changes in white segregation were not associated with changes in the size of the black population. The residential preferences literature suggests that whites tend to be more averse to blacks than to others;[17] if aversion to other groups was the sole factor producing segregation, we might expect that changes in the African American population would have had the largest effect.

In any case, the implication of these findings is that while greater diversity does not translate into greater integration, it could facilitate integration in certain circumstances, such as for African Americans. Conversely, greater diversity can increase segregation, at least in the short run, if diversity is propelled by the growth of immigration and ethnic enclaves.

NEIGHBORHOOD INTEGRATION
AND NEIGHBORHOOD STABILITY

Ingrid Gould Ellen has written extensively about the integration and stability of neighborhoods. On the occasion of the fiftieth anniversary of the Supreme Court's *Brown v. Board of Education* decision, she observed that "the popular press has been filled with stories lamenting the unfulfilled promise of the case. One article after another describes how segregated our schools remain along racial and ethnic lines. But while we've seen little progress in school integration in recent decades, neighborhoods in the United States have been quietly and steadily growing more integrated. . . . Although levels of residential segregation remain undeniably high, this emphasis on segregation can obscure the fact that integrated communities do exist and, as one of the key findings here demonstrates, are becoming more, not less, common."[18]

Until recently, work on neighborhoods generally assumed the unavoidability of racial turnover, particularly in the two-group—black-white—context. Ellen relates the often-quoted line by Saul Alinsky, a community organizer in the middle decades of the twentieth century, that racial integration is merely the "time between when the first black moves in and the last white moves out."[19] The "invasion and succession" model was more formally articulated by Otis Dudley and Beverly Duncan, who described the near inevitability of resegregation following the entry of blacks into white neighborhoods.[20]

By the 1970s, there were indications that at least some integrated neighborhoods were relatively stable. In a study relying on data from 1970 and 1980, Nancy Denton and Douglas Massey, for example, found that all-white neighborhoods had become rarer, and the simple presence of racial or ethnic minorities in small numbers no longer precipitated rapid neighborhood turnover. They did emphasize, however, that white population loss was greater in diverse neighborhoods.[21] Other studies indicated that stability was more common in smaller cities of the South and West that had smaller black populations, perhaps where racial integration did not threaten the ability of whites to maintain low levels of contact with blacks.[22] The increase in stability was also consistent with a shift in white racial attitudes, where a greater proportion of whites accepted, at least in principle, open housing.

Ellen analyzed the issue of stability with more recent data by categorizing neighborhoods by their racial and ethnic composition. She classified some neighborhoods as ethnically homogeneous, others as "integrated," and yet others as "mixed minority." In her scheme, an integrated neighborhood is one where non-Hispanic whites make up 40 percent or more of the population, and at least one minority group accounts for at least 10 percent of the population. She notes that she purposefully used the presence of whites in this definition because "it is whites who have historically excluded (and avoided) members of minority groups. Thus while a neighborhood shared by blacks, Hispanics, and Asians may be wonderfully diverse, it is not considered integrated [in this analysis]."[23] She therefore defined neighborhoods shared by multiple minority groups but with relatively few whites as "mixed minority."

Figure 17 shows the distribution of neighborhoods across all metropolitan areas in the United States by their racial composition in the

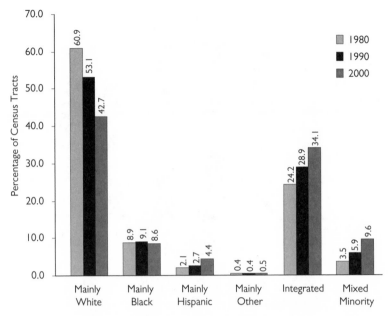

FIGURE 17. Racial composition of neighborhoods in all U.S. metropolitan areas, 1980–2000. Source: Ingrid Gould Ellen (2007), "How Integrated Did We Become during the 1990s?" in *Fragile Rights within Cities: Government, Housing, and Fairness*, ed. John Goering (Lanham, MD: Rowman and Littlefield), 131.

1980 to 2000 period covered by Ellen's study. The figure shows that the proportion of neighborhoods that were mainly white fell substantially from nearly 61 percent in 1980 to less than 43 percent in 2000. While about a quarter of all neighborhoods were integrated in 1980, by 2000 this number rose to just over a third. The proportion of neighborhoods that were mixed minority also grew over the period, to nearly 10 percent in 2000. Other studies using somewhat different typologies of integration have found similar results. For example, David Fasenfest, Jason Booza, and Kurt Metzger, in a study of the ten largest metropolitan areas in the United States, found that the number of predominately white neighborhoods fell by 30 percent in the 1990s, and nine of the ten metropolitan areas saw an increase in mixed-race neighborhoods.[24]

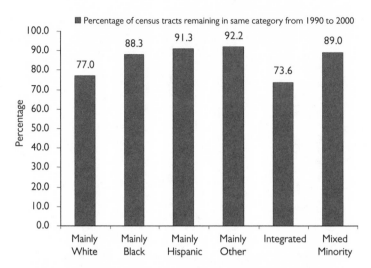

FIGURE 18. Racial change by type of neighborhood in all U.S. metropolitan areas, 1990–2000. Source: Ingrid Gould Ellen (2007), "How Integrated Did We Become during the 1990s?" in *Fragile Rights within Cities: Government, Housing, and Fairness,* ed. John Goering (Lanham, MD: Rowman and Littlefield), 133.

Put yet another way, in 2000, the average white individual in a U.S. metropolitan area lived in a census tract where 20 percent of the residents were nonwhite or Hispanic—up from 15 percent in 1990 and 12 percent in 1980.[25]

Figure 18 shows the stability of different types of neighborhoods. It indicates that there is a fair amount of stability in integrated neighborhoods, though such neighborhoods are generally not as stable as ethnically homogeneous ones. While 77 percent of neighborhoods that were mainly white in 1990 stayed as such in 2000, and 88.3 to 92.2 percent of mainly black, Hispanic, and "other" neighborhoods did the same, a somewhat more modest 73.6 percent of integrated neighborhoods in 1990 remained integrated in 2000.

Ethnographic research by Michael Maly supports some of these findings. His book *Beyond Segregation* focuses on the growing prominence of neighborhoods experiencing stable integration. The heart of the book consists of three neighborhood case studies: Uptown in Chicago, Jackson Heights in New York City, and San Antonio–Fruitvale in Oakland. Maly discusses the local racial and ethnic tensions in these neighborhoods, challenges faced by residents, and ultimately the collaborative efforts by some multiethnic community organizations to address common issues, such as commercial revitalization, youth development, and image maintenance. These joint community efforts often then help sustain stable integration.[26] In this same vein, in a study of neighborhood stability, change, and intergroup conflict in a few Chicago neighborhoods, William Julius Wilson and Richard Taub conclude that neighborhood stability is greatest in areas where there are strong local social organizations, such as school councils, business associations, and civic leagues. They report that in Chicago neighborhoods lacking these organizations, stability was elusive, and invasion-succession was the dominant pattern.[27]

When breaking integrated neighborhoods down into white-black, white-Hispanic, white-other, and white-multiethnic neighborhoods, Ellen finds less stability in the retention of those precise ethnic balances (as opposed to retaining the broader label "integrated") over the 1990s. For example, 63 percent of white-black neighborhoods in 1990 remained white-black by 2000. The corresponding figures for stability among white-Hispanic, white-other, and white-multiethnic neighborhoods were 59 percent, 66 percent, and 44 percent. Thus, stability is least common in neighborhoods that are specifically white-multiethnic.[28]

Notably, Ellen also finds that most neighborhoods that became integrated in the 1990s were principally those that began the decade as mainly white. The implication is that neighborhoods tend to be integrated by minorities moving into white communities rather than whites moving into minority neighborhoods, such as through gentrification. Research by John Logan and Charles Zhang largely confirms this. They find that whites are less likely to enter minority neighborhoods and that diversity generally results when minorities enter white neighborhoods.

They further note that diversity can be reversed, usually by the movement of whites out of such multiethnic neighborhoods.[29]

There are a number of mixed-race neighborhoods in Washington, D.C., itself. In *Turf Wars*, a rich ethnographic account of the Mt. Pleasant neighborhood in the city, Gabriella Gahlia Modan describes how the neighborhood was primarily middle-class majority white in the early half of the twentieth century. It then transitioned into a middle-class majority African American neighborhood in the 1950s following desegregation and the subsequent flight of whites. However, the area became more ethnically diverse when young professionals, mainly white, began moving into the area in the late 1970s. Around this time, immigrants from the Caribbean, Central America, and East Africa also began to move in. Modan describes "the mid-to-late 1990s [as] a turning point in the process of gentrification that *commodified* the ethnic diversity of the neighborhood, turning ethnic diversity into a feature that brought added symbolic value to living there and added economic value to real estate prices."[30]

That is, diversity was being marketed as a distinctive and attractive feature for prospective residents. This is in line with research by Richard Florida showing that population diversity often attracts artists ("bohemians"), creative individuals, and other highly skilled professionals.[31] Indeed, neighborhood diversity appeared to be highly valued by a number of residents in Modan's study. For example, as one person interviewed described the Mt. Pleasant neighborhood: "I think the operative word is, diverse. It's diverse in terms of economics, in terms of races, um, you got—gay couples living next to, families, and, you know—you name it, th—the reason I was attracted to it when I first came to Washington, I'm from New York, and it was the only part of Washington that, at all reminded me of New York. And—the reason it did was because it's diverse."[32]

Modan nevertheless also discusses how the current and future identity of Mt. Pleasant remains contested, as not all residents share a common set of goals. From the mid-1990s through the mid-2000s, rents and home-ownership costs (including property taxes) continued to go up, pricing some low-income residents out of the neighborhood. Thus, while the area today remains ethnically diverse, this does not mean it will inevitably stay that way in the coming years.[33]

Ellen similarly concludes that while the number of exclusively white neighborhoods has fallen and the number of fairly stable integrated neighborhoods has risen, there are reasons to be cautious about concluding that stable and equitable integration is the predominate feature of American residential life. For one, there has been relatively little change in the prevalence of neighborhoods shared by whites and blacks—integration is mainly fueled by whites sharing neighborhoods with Hispanics and Asians. Second, while the stability of integrated neighborhoods increased from the 1970s to the 1980s, there was little change in the stability in the 1990s. Third, white households with children were among the least likely to live in integrated neighborhoods and the most likely to avoid them. This is consistent with evidence indicating little decline in school segregation in the 1990s.[34] Ellen speculates that many white households with children hold negative views about the quality of public schools in integrated areas and thus eschew living in such areas.[35]

DIVERSITY AND THE QUALITY
OF GROUP RELATIONS

While the number and stability of diverse neighborhoods have grown, what is less clear is the quality of intergroup interactions in these areas. That is, just because multiple groups live in close proximity does not necessarily mean that relations between groups are congenial or even cordial. There are two common theoretical perspectives concerning the effects of diversity on social connections. The "contact theory" holds that diversity fosters interethnic familiarity and tolerance. As members of groups get to know each other better, they get along better and trust each other more. In contrast, "conflict theory" argues that, for various reasons, such as the competition for power and other scarce resources, diversity fosters distrust between groups and strengthens relationships within groups.[36]

Robert Putnam has argued that in the short run immigration and diversity tend to reduce social solidarity and social capital, which in some ways supports conflict theory. For example, he found that in very diverse cities like Los Angeles, Houston, and Yakima, Washington, residents were considerably less likely to report that they trust their neighbors than in more homogeneous places like Bismarck, North Dakota, or Fremont, Michigan. However, Putnam's story is more complex. Not only do residents of all races in ethnically diverse neighborhoods exhibit lower levels of trust of other groups, they are also more likely to "hunker down" and show lower levels of trust of people of their own ethnicity. In diverse areas, altruism and community cooperation are less common; people report having fewer friends and demonstrate lower confidence in local government.[37]

Thus, conflict theory does not fully explain what is going on, because diversity is not strengthening within-group ties. Putnam argues that diversity more generally triggers anomie or social isolation and that diversity is associated with withdrawal from collective life. In addition, others argue that people's social worlds are not as spatially defined as they used to be, resulting in less need to interact with actual neighbors. "Through telephones, computers, and automobiles," write Richard Alba and Nancy Denton, "immigrant ethnics are able to maintain connections to kin and co-ethnics who may live at some distance from them, even in their country of origin."[38]

A 2007 *Washington Post* article describing the new movement of Hispanics to largely African American neighborhoods in the southeastern part of Washington, D.C., illustrates this. The reporter asked German and Elsy Ramos, originally from El Salvador, about the quality of their interactions in their new neighborhood. The couple said they did not really talk to their neighbors, partly because they did not speak much English. "We haven't any problems with the neighbors," Elsy

Ramos told the *Post* in Spanish. "We're inside. They do their thing; we don't get involved with them. You have to get along with your neighbors, but you don't have to interfere in their lives."[39] Similarly, in a study of some Houston apartment complexes, Nestor Rodriguez describes how African Americans and Hispanics share common residential space but live culturally and socially apart. For example, Latinos make extensive use of the local soccer field, while African Americans are more likely to congregate on the basketball court.[40]

Diverse neighborhoods are also at times sites of outright conflict between groups. Returning to Modan's book *Turf Wars*, we see that neighbors in Mt. Pleasant struggle over local resources and the authority to determine what kinds of activities are appropriate and allowable in the public spaces—streets and parks—of the neighborhood. These issues are further complicated by the overlap between ethnicity and class. Some more-affluent white residents tend to be more concerned about keeping streets clean and safe, while lower-income Latino residents resent these efforts as an imposition of social control, for example, the attempt to prevent loitering by posting signs in Spanish that target and marginalize Latinos.[41]

Conflict between minority groups also occurs in diverse areas, such as between Hispanics and blacks in Los Angeles, where residential succession has been occurring in many neighborhoods that have a history of a strong black presence (such as South Central Los Angeles). Some blacks in these areas express concern about sharing social services and losing control of local institutions. Hispanics for their part complain about a lack of access to municipal jobs and leadership positions in local government.[42] The 1992 Los Angeles riots, in which many Korean-owned stores were destroyed, also exposed the deep strains between Korean entrepreneurs and some African Americans in the inner city.

However, as Nancy Foner and George Frederickson note, "Interethnic and racial relations, of course, are not all about conflict."[43] In their edited volume, John Li argues that media attention often enflames local tensions and underplays the peaceful coexistence between groups. It is not that conflict is absent, but rather that there is a greater heterogeneity in individual interactions than often depicted.[44] In Compton, where there is indeed competition between blacks and Latinos over issues of political representation, there are also examples of cooperation and coalition building, such as in joint efforts to keep local streets clean and free of crime and drugs.[45] Michael Maly similarly describes how multiethnic collaborative efforts by community organizations, while sometimes marked by intergroup squabbling, nevertheless have succeeded in addressing common issues, such as providing more services for local youth in San Antonio–Fruitvale, California.[46]

Certainly, data on friendships and intermarriage rates tend to support the notion that ethnic relations are often amiable. About 30 percent of Hispanics and 20 percent of Asians marry non-Hispanics and non-Asians, respectively. Moreover, it has been estimated that while out-marriage rates are about 8 percent among first-generation Hispanics, this rises to 32 percent among the second generation, and 57 percent for the third generation. Similarly, out-marriage rates are 13 percent among first-generation Asians, 34 percent among the second generation, and 54 percent among the third.[47] Other research indicates that U.S.-born Mexican-origin people are also more involved in cross-ethnic ties than Mexican immigrants, which is consistent with greater social integration over time.[48]

Again, this is not to overlook the extent of racial and ethnic conflict in the United States. At the very least, it appears that ethnic conflict is more intense when there is a strong overlap between ethnicity and socioeconomic status (as is often the case). Modan explicitly describes how the conflict between ethnic groups in the Mt. Pleasant neighborhood is often compounded by class. Whites in the neighborhood are more likely to be wealthier home owners, and they often articulate positions about the uses of public and private space that are correlated with class, as described above.[49]

Putnam, who provided a rather dim picture of current interethnic relations in diverse areas, argues that in the long run, successful immigrant societies overcome divisions by creating new forms of social solidarity, often as people forge broader identities. For example, deep divisions between religious groups in the United States, such as Protestants and Catholics in the nineteenth and through the middle decades of the twentieth century, diminished over time. Greater experience of living in diverse areas, along with rising marriage rates across racial and ethnic lines, may mean that future generations may feel less discomfort with ethnic diversity, and ethnicity itself may become a less salient and more symbolic feature of self-identification.[50] Whether this will be the case in the United States in coming years remains to be seen.

THE SEGREGATION
OF MULTIRACIAL INDIVIDUALS

Racial and ethnic intermarriage is often thought to be one of the quintessential indicators of "structural assimilation," in that high levels of intermarriage both reflect and further contribute to low levels of social distance between groups. Indeed, intermarriage tends to occur more frequently among groups that are less residentially segregated. For example, Asian-white intermarriage is more common and residential segregation between these groups is considerably lower than black-white intermarriage and segregation.[51]

Relatively little research has been conducted on the segregation of multiracial individuals from various other groups. It was only with the 2000 census that individuals participating in government surveys could report more than one race. Complicating the issue is the fact that information on Hispanic origin is collected separately from information on "race," such that those counted as "multiracial" individuals do not typically include those who are Hispanic and, say, white, or black, or Asian. Rather, the census count of multiracial individuals typically includes people who marked more than one of the following: white, black, one of a number of Asian groups, American Indian, and "some other race." In 2005, just under 2 percent of the population reported two or more

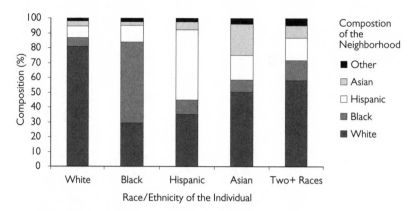

FIGURE 19. Average neighborhood ethnic composition for all U.S. metropolitan areas, 2000. Source: William H. Frey and Dowell Myers (2002), "Neighborhood Segregation in Single-Race and Multirace America: A Census 2000 Study of Cities and Metropolitan Areas," Fannie Mae Foundation Working Paper, www.censusscope.org/FreyWPFinal.pdf (retrieved June 18, 2007), 10.

races using these definitions.[52] This number may grow in the future with the increasing frequency of racial intermarriage.

In a study of the multiracial population, William Frey and Dowell Meyers show that people identifying as two or more races tend to live in diverse neighborhoods (see figure 19). They also found that people who report two or more races are relatively less segregated from non-Hispanic whites than are blacks, Asians, or Hispanics (see figure 20). For example, the multiracial-white dissimilarity score, at 0.33, was lower than the Hispanic-white, Asian-white, or black-white scores. The dissimilarity score of multiracial individuals who reported being black and white from non-Hispanic whites, at 0.51, was lower than the black-white dissimilarity score (0.59). Unlike blacks, multiracial individuals who reported being black and white also lived in neighborhoods that were, on average, majority white. The dissimilarity score for multiracial individuals who reported being Asian and white from non-Hispanic

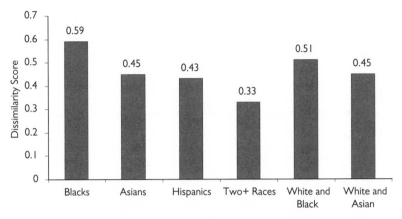

FIGURE 20. Mean indices of dissimilarity from non-Hispanic whites in major U.S. metropolitan areas, 2000. Source: William H. Frey and Dowell Myers (2002), "Neighborhood Segregation in Single-Race and Multirace America: A Census 2000 Study of Cities and Metropolitan Areas," Fannie Mae Foundation Working Paper, www.censusscope.org/FreyWPFinal.pdf (retrieved June 18, 2007), 36–41.

whites, however, did not differ from the Asian-white dissimilarity score (both 0.45).[53]

These findings are generally consistent with research by Steven Holloway and his coauthors on mixed-race households using 1990 census data. They found that mixed-race households were more likely to live in diverse neighborhoods than same-race white households, though in less diverse areas than same-race nonwhite households, mainly because Asians and Hispanics often live in diverse areas as it is. Black-white households also lived in more diverse neighborhoods than the black population in general. Halloway and his coauthors conclude that "the empirical analysis produces the impression of the 'in-betweenness' of the residential geography of mixed-race partnerships . . . these households are not found exclusively in the neighborhood terrain of one group or the other. Instead there is some evidence of their congregation in diverse local settings."[54]

In 2002 the *Washington Post* interviewed a number of local families about these issues. Members of the Interracial Family Circle, a Washington, D.C.–area group of multiracial residents, for example, reported the pros and cons of different neighborhoods. According to Nancy Leigh Knox, the group's president, multiracial families made decisions about where to live differently than single-race families. "People want to be where it's diverse," Knox said. "Everyone talks about it as being the primary criterion."[55]

Likewise, one of the people Modan interviewed in *Turf Wars* described how, "For our daughter, it's very important [as a black-white biracial child] to have . . . access to all kinds of people. . . . I think that's the strength of the neighborhood. We wanted a mixed race, mixed income kind of community. . . . You know—having your kid grow up in a place that, um, where everybody's the same, and they aren't one of those same, creates weird identity issues."[56]

Indeed, in the Washington, D.C., metropolitan area, people who were counted in the 2000 census as being both black and white typically lived in a neighborhood that was 54 percent white and 27 percent black. In contrast, white residents lived in neighborhoods that were on average 72 percent white and 26 percent black, and the typical neighborhood for a black person was 12 percent white and 60 percent black. Figures also indicated that individuals who were Asian-only did not live in neighborhoods vastly different from those of individuals who reported being both Asian and white.[57] Thus, because Asians and Hispanics often live in more diverse neighborhoods, the issue of living in a diverse area appears to be more salient for multiracial black and white households.

CONCLUSIONS

The analysis in this chapter suggests that increasing diversity is associated with decreasing segregation among African Americans. This is consistent with the notion that the presence of other minority groups, and Hispanics in particular, may serve as a "buffer" between whites and blacks, resulting in less segregation between blacks and other groups. Multiethnic metropolitan areas are also often newer areas in the South and West with less historically entrenched black ghettos. Nevertheless, increases in diversity are associated with increases in the segregation of whites, Hispanics, and Asians from other groups. It is mainly the growth of the Hispanic and Asian populations in particular that is associated with growing Hispanic and Asian segregation, respectively. This affirms the notion that continued high levels of immigration may be increasing segregation of these groups at least in the short run—as new arrivals are often the most segregated from other groups—even as the native-born of these groups tend to live in more integrated communities.

That white segregation from other groups declined over the 1980–2000 period despite growing diversity (i.e., segregation declined less in places with the largest increases in diversity) suggests a couple of alternative explanations. On the one hand, the finding is consistent with the hypothesis that whites are averse to living in more diverse areas. On the other hand, it could also be that forces producing the positive association between Asian and Hispanic segregation from others—the inflow of many recent immigrants who tend to display higher levels of segregation—is also serving to, at least in the short run, produce greater white segregation from others in these diverse areas.

On the subject of neighborhood integration and stability, the review of recent research indicates that the number of diverse neighborhoods is increasing, and many of these are also more stable in their racial and ethnic composition than was the case in the past. Yet while the number of exclusively white neighborhoods has substantially fallen and the number of stable integrated neighborhoods has risen, there are reasons to be cautious about concluding that most diverse neighborhoods will remain so in the future. Many integrated neighborhoods likely continue to change over a longer period of time, and whites appear to be less likely to move into integrated neighborhoods. In addition, white households with children are among the least likely to live in integrated neighborhoods, and the most likely to avoid them, perhaps due to apprehensions—real or perceived—about school quality.

The quality of intergroup relations in diverse areas also varies widely. Research by Robert Putnam indicates that in the short run immigration and diversity tend to reduce social solidarity and social capital, even among people of the same race. He reports that in diverse areas people are more likely to "hunker down" and withdraw from public life. In other contexts, diversity produces intense conflict between groups. Yet in others, people pull together through community efforts to enhance local goods and services that improve the life of all community members. It seems reasonable to conclude that conflict is more intense when class compounds ethnic difference. For example, in a gentrifying neighborhood with affluent whites and poor minorities, there are often conflicting visions about the use of public space and community resources.

Finally, concerning the residential segregation of multiracial individuals, research indicates that multiracial people generally live in more diverse neighborhoods than whites or blacks. This finding is consistent with spatial assimilation. It appears that multiracial households often deliberately seek out diverse areas where their children may experience less dissonance than if they lived in mostly homogeneous areas.

What, then, can we say about the effects of growing diversity? Certainly, diversity opens opportunities for both conflict and cooperation. One can find numerous examples of each in communities across the country, as shown in the newspaper stories that opened this chapter. In the first, we saw a local nonprofit organization working to aid the stable integration of newcomers. In the second, where a naturalized citizen originally from the Philippines was seeking a seat on the county Board of Supervisors, we saw some allusions to group tension but not really to hostility. The story exemplified an attempt to work through the system to bring about orderly and incremental change. The third article, about the elderly couple who complained about the new immigrants in their subdivision, illustrated more overt antipathy. The couple's decision to move exemplified the invasion-succession process that sometimes produces racial and ethnic turnover in neighborhoods.

In the short run, the change in group dynamics that accompanies demographic change often produces some growth in residential segregation and group conflict. There may be competing visions about the form and direction of local organizations and institutions. The analyses in this chapter suggest that the group that may have benefited most from diversity in terms of their isolation from others is African Americans. After all, due to a history of intense racism and discrimination, this is a group that hardly benefited from the status quo. Growing demographic diversity may, in small ways, reduce the stark black-white residential divide in many metropolitan areas.

The longer-run implications of growing diversity for residential patterns, of course, remain to be seen. There are reasons to believe that high levels of residential segregation will not persist, as indicated by analyses in previous chapters. High rates of intermarriage across generations, and the residential patterns displayed by multiracial individuals, suggest that diversity will result not necessarily in a residentially polarized society but in one where many groups of people share, with some degree of both harmony and conflict, communal space.

CHAPTER 7

Conclusion

In this book I have explored how immigration to the United States is reshaping the metropolitan landscape. Through an examination of residential segregation patterns, my goal was to answer the following questions: Is there evidence that immigrants are residentially assimilating? Does the assimilation process look very different for immigrants of different racial and ethnic backgrounds? How do other characteristics of immigrants, such as English-language fluency and socioeconomic standing, affect the extent of residential segregation? What has been the impact of immigration on the segregation patterns of native-born blacks and whites? How stable are diverse neighborhoods and what is the quality of group relations in them?

The analyses herein show that immigrants are by and large becoming residentially assimilated in American metropolitan areas. Native-born Hispanics, Asians, and blacks are all less segregated from whites than are the foreign-born of these groups. Immigrants who have been in the United States for longer periods of time are also generally less segregated than new arrivals. Socioeconomic differences play an important role in explaining patterns and trends for all racial and ethnic groups—especially for Hispanics and Asians. Those of higher socioeconomic status are substantially less segregated from whites than lower-socioeconomic-status individuals. These findings support the notion that over time we may see greater integration if and as a larger proportion of these groups move up the socioeconomic ladder in the coming years. Indeed, research on the economic incorporation of immigrants generally shows that immigrant educational attainment and income levels rise over time and across generations, though among some Latino groups the gap with non-Hispanic whites does not disappear.[1]

A second conclusion is that in many cases we are witnessing *multiple* forms of assimilation. For example, some analyses indicate that we see a pattern of residential assimilation of Hispanics not only with native-born non-Hispanic whites (Anglos) but also with African Americans. Moreover, Hispanic race groups also show particularly low levels of segregation from native-born Hispanics not of their own race, indicating the salience of pan-Hispanic identity that crosses racial boundaries. In diverse societies it is therefore important to recognize that particular groups can experience a reduction in differences from any number of other groups.

Ethnographic studies in New York show some of the same patterns among Asian immigrant groups. Among the Chinese and Korean second generation, some have observed the emergence of an "Asian" identity, whereby some Chinese and Korean youth occasionally worship together, live in close proximity, and join similar political groups.[2] At the same time, many children of upwardly mobile immigrant Asian parents are also assimilating into the broader middle-class society. As Dae Young Kim writes: "The American-born or -raised children of Korean immigrants arguably benefited from residential integration: they grew up in middle-class white neighborhoods and attended excellent suburban schools. . . . With educational credentials that presented very few obstacles in the current labor market, second-generation Korean Americans entered the mainstream very rapidly." Kim is careful to note that ethnicity may reassert itself if Koreans face a glass ceiling in corporate America, or if continued immigration or transnationalism reinforces ethnic identity in the future.[3]

A third conclusion is that the extent and pace of spatial assimilation among immigrants are nevertheless still substantially shaped by race and ethnicity. For example, levels of segregation from native-born non-Hispanic whites are very high among black immigrants and relatively low among white immigrants. Hispanic and Asian immigrants fall in between. Moreover, "assimilation" does not always suggest the same type of process for all groups. For example, among racially diverse Hispanic immigrants, those who identify as white or other-race are considerably less segregated from non-Hispanic whites than those who report being black. Conversely, for black Hispanic immigrants, assimilation may mean slight declines in segregation from whites over time and across generations, but even larger declines in segregation from non-Hispanic blacks. In fact, the very high overall segregation levels of black Hispanics and black immigrants more generally from Anglos tend to overshadow the slight generational convergence. Some of the findings here are thus as consistent with segmented assimilation as with spatial assimilation. That is, immigrant groups to some extent experience divergent patterns of incorporation into the United States depending on their race and ethnicity.

COLOR LINES REVISITED

One of the major issues raised by increasing immigration and the resulting diversity is the possible impact these trends have on the U.S. color line. The analyses here suggest that we may see racial and ethnic boundary "blurring" in the coming years. For example, there is evidence of low to moderate levels of segregation among Hispanic subgroups, suggesting the salience of Hispanic pan-ethnicity. We also see the attenuation of segregation between non-black Hispanics in particular and whites. Moderate levels of Asian-white segregation and high rates of Asian out-marriage with whites also suggest relatively low levels of social distance between these groups.

Interestingly, growing diversity in metropolitan America, fueled by immigration, has also had important implications for the historically unyielding color line between whites and blacks. Immigration has likely softened the rigid black-white divide, as black segregation from others, including whites, tends to be lower in multiethnic metropolitan areas. While the reasons for this are not entirely clear, it may be that having multiple minority groups in a metropolitan area may moderate the single minority versus white majority thinking that dominated in the past. Because of immigration, whites are also now considerably less likely to live in all-white neighborhoods than previously. While the sharing of residential space does not in itself necessarily result in greater intergroup harmony—and in fact sometimes leads to considerable conflict—such exposure does sometimes produce multiracial coalitions built on shared interests. For example, groups often share the goal of living in safe neighborhoods with satisfactory housing and good public education, and they work together toward these ends.

More generally, high rates of intermarriage between ethnic groups suggest that immigrants and their offspring are for the most part becoming socially incorporated in the United States. Despite a number of significant differences in the context of reception between the great wave of immigration in the late nineteenth and early twentieth centuries and today's wave, we still see some similarity in the patterns of incorporation. For example, Joel Perlmann and Mary Waters compared current patterns of Mexican intermarriage with those of Italians in the early to middle decades of the twentieth century. Intermarriage is thought to be one of the quintessential indicators of assimilation (or structural assimilation), given that it involves intimate relations between individuals of different ethnic groups. Perlmann and Waters conclude that out-marriage patterns do not differ much between Italians of then and Mexicans of now. The researchers are careful to note the differences in today's context that prevent them from concluding that Mexican assimilation is inevitable, such as the continuation of large-scale immigration from Mexico (as opposed to the cessation of immigration from Italy after the 1920s). Nevertheless, their findings suggest that a significant proportion of fourth- and fifth-generation descendants of the Hispanic and Asian immigrants of today will be of mixed origins.[4]

Perlmann and Waters also point out that having children outside of marriage is much more common today than a century ago. This is salient because, as research by David Harris and Hiromi Ono has shown, cohabiters of all races are also more likely to be in cross-racial and ethnic relationships than married couples. For example, the percentage of white women's partners who are Asian is twice as high among cohabiters as among married couples. About double the proportion of black men cohabit with white women as are married to them. Harris and Ono conclude that "there are substantially higher levels of intimate interracial contact than marriage data imply, and consequently that the social distance between racial groups is less than previous work suggests."[5]

In addition, a high proportion of births in general occur outside of marriage. In 2000, 22 percent of births among non-Hispanic whites were attributed to unmarried mothers, as were 69 percent of births among non-Hispanic black mothers and 43 percent of births among Hispanic mothers. The patterns for the ethnic identity of children of interracial couples—especially unmarried couples—is not well known or understood. Perlmann and Waters thus conclude that "how changes in cohabitation, divorce, and childbearing come to affect interethnic commingling and resultant ethnic and racial identity in the next generation are big issues for the future understanding of ethnic blending."[6]

The findings from the current study that suggest the importance of considering multiple and concurrent forms of assimilation and incorporation are consistent with research suggesting that the younger generation, particularly those of mixed origins, have less rigid identities. Philip Kasinitz refers to this as part of a "hybrid culture" evident among many children of immigrants. He notes that "the content and boundaries of these new identities [of the second generation] also seem to be in flux." Some among the second generation adopt pan-ethnic identities, which are to some extent racialized, but this could be just a "station on the road to total incorporation."[7] Kasinitz further notes that "the current discussion of second-generation incorporation also often sounds is if there is one clearly defined majority culture into which people do or do not 'assimilate.' Of course, we know things are more complicated than that. The cultural and political life of New York, Los Angeles, and Miami has been transformed by immigrants, even as the immigrants are transformed themselves. It is really not a question of 'preserving traditions' versus 'becoming American.'"[8] Kasinitz does not mean to imply that there is no color line; the young immigrants he and his colleagues studied also recount experiencing discrimination at the hands of both whites and other ethnic groups.[9] Nevertheless, he hypothesizes that the popular culture of the younger generation may be turning it into something more varied and dynamic.

Frank Bean and his coauthors likewise note that the new diversity in America is "likely eroding color lines, although less for blacks than others, and that the matter of race in America may be more dynamic than ever."[10] They cite the high proportion of Asians and Latinos with a spouse of another race, with a vast majority married to a white partner, and the higher proportion of younger people who identify as being multiracial.[11] Furthermore, racial identification among individuals of mixed marriages is often flexible, as they identify themselves in different ways at different times and in different situations. For example, one study found that about 12 percent of youths participating in a longitudinal survey provided inconsistent responses to nearly identical questions about race at the different times they were interviewed.[12] It is quite possible that the multiracial population could account for one-fifth of the nation's population by the year 2050, though any projection this far into the future is speculative.[13]

ACKNOWLEDGING UNPREDICTABILITY

Despite these trends, I nevertheless remain cautious about asserting the inevitability of spatial assimilation of immigrants into American neighborhoods and the blurring of the color line. First, as emphasized in chapters 4 and 5, despite some moderate declines in black segregation over the past few decades, native-born and immigrant blacks continue to be more segregated from whites than other groups. The historical black-white divide in American society, and the continued—albeit declining—discrimination against blacks in the housing market still play important roles in shaping residential patterns. It is also easy to find examples of continuing conflict between various ethnic groups across American communities, as discussed in chapter 6. Whether the long-run trend of moderate declines in black segregation continues, and eventually translates into less polarization and greater integration for black immigrants and their children, will be an important issue to track in the coming years.

Second, as noted in several chapters, that acculturation indicators (such as English-language fluency) and socioeconomic characteristics often help explain relatively high levels of segregation among some groups—and among Hispanic immigrants in particular—also has important implications. On the one hand, this suggests that spatial assimilation processes are at work that could reduce segregation over the longer run as Hispanics achieve economic upward mobility. On the other hand, high levels of Hispanic immigration, largely consisting of people of low socioeconomic status—precisely the characteristics associated with high levels of segregation—suggest that we should in fact witness increasing levels of segregation for Hispanics in the short and medium term.

Because of high levels of immigration, Hispanics, and to a lesser extent Asians, are now living in neighborhoods with more coethnics than before. In the short term, at least, immigration is fortifying ethnic communities in U.S. metropolitan areas. If there were to be some kind of negative economic, political, or social disturbance that either inhibited future Hispanic socioeconomic mobility or heightened tensions between Hispanics and other groups, then segregation might increase. For example, if we see growing income inequality coupled with a decline in social mobility in the coming years, this could spell the growth of a distinct Hispanic underclass. Similarly, continued Hispanic immigration, and the growth of the undocumented population in particular, could continue to provoke a reaction in the U.S.-born population that could likewise stigmatize Hispanics and heighten social tension and discrimination, reinforcing residential segregation over the longer run.[14]

LOOKING TO THE FUTURE: RESEARCH AND POLICY

In light of these conclusions, there are a number of areas where future research would be useful. First, while various government surveys, such as the decennial census (the main source of data in the analyses of segregation patterns), cover undocumented immigrants in the survey effort, such immigrants are undoubtedly undercounted. Even when they are counted, the census, for good reason, does not ask individuals about their legal status. Thus, we know relatively little about the residential patterns and patterns of social and economic incorporation of the undocumented population. It is estimated that about half of Hispanics in the United States are foreign-born, among whom roughly 40 percent are undocumented.[15] One might reasonably hypothesize that undocumented immigrants are not particularly well residentially integrated, given their relatively low levels of income and education, their lack of legal rights, and their vulnerability to deportation and exploitation.

Likewise, it would be useful to study the effects of any new immigration policy. For example, it is reasonable to hypothesize that the implementation of a large guest-worker program would increase the segregation of immigrants, at least in the short run. While there may be some short-term economic reasons for instituting a guest-worker program, the admittance of a large number of temporary, low-skill workers with relatively few rights or prospects for legal incorporation through citizenship would likely mean the growth of a socially, economically, and politically marginalized constituency. The record of guest-worker programs in other liberal democracies, such as Germany, indicates that it is unlikely that all immigrants who have spent a few years in the United States will simply leave when their work visas expire. A significant proportion of current undocumented immigrants in the United States are in fact visa overstayers (one estimate being 25 to 40 percent of undocumented immigrants) rather than people who crossed the border illegally.[16]

On the other hand, policies that favor admitting a higher proportion of immigrants on the basis of skills, rather than on family reunification grounds, could serve to reduce segregation. Immigrants who are professionals, such as scientists and engineers, tend to rely less on ethnic networks and more on the ties they develop with particular employers, which might have been the sources of their visas.[17] In contrast, people who immigrate on the basis of family reunification already have ties to kin in the United States and are probably more likely to settle with them. Of course, it should be said that immigration policy should not be shaped only on the basis on its short-term effect on residential segregation patterns. Immigration policy has long had an important humanitarian component that should continue to inform policy decisions.

Future research should also continue to track trends in racial and ethnic intermarriage and the patterns of ethnic identification among children of mixed marriages and mixed nonmarital unions. Information about these trends will provide insight into the trajectory of the color line, as discussed above. How rigid are people's identities? How will patterns of identification change in the context of an increasingly diverse society?

A related theme meriting continued attention is whether we will witness either a more general black-nonblack divide in race relations (one that features unique levels of disadvantage among blacks), a white-nonwhite divide (where whites are uniquely privileged), or perhaps neither (where we see attenuation of difference among all groups). While it is clear that the pace of incorporation and the extent of inequality experienced by various groups differ—much as they did among white immigrant groups of the past century—it is important for the study of future race relations to gauge whether there is a dominant trend in the color line's trajectory.

In order to better understand the immigrant integration process, it is also important to gain greater understanding about how the context of reception affects patterns of incorporation. For example, it is not sufficient to document whether assimilation is a dominant trend in a particular country or locale. After all, it is not difficult to find areas both within countries and across countries that are examples of successful incorporation and unsuccessful incorporation. Rather, what are the most important factors that set the two outcomes apart? What is the role of the local economic context? For example, what are the implications of growing economic inequality for immigrant adaptation? Does intergenerational economic mobility help reduce the potentially harmful effects of inequality? Do social expectations about immigrant acculturation (for example, English-only policies) and accompanying programs (such as English-language classes) bolster assimilation? Or does multiculturalism in fact facilitate immigrant incorporation by allowing immigrants to express themselves and in turn reduce their social alienation? Is there an appropriate balance between the two? Of course, whether U.S. policy should in fact promote assimilation is in the end based on people's values about whether assimilation is a desirable goal.

Finally, it would be helpful to monitor how immigrant adaptation in one dimension affects incorporation in another. For example, how strongly is economic incorporation associated with structural assimilation (as indicated by, say, patterns of intermarriage), and will these patterns change in the future? Will spatial assimilation lead to greater political assimilation, say in terms of civic engagement and participation in the political process? What are the appropriate markers for "successful" immigrant adaptation and incorporation?

In the residential sphere, there are reasons to be interested in residential segregation between ethnic groups (the main focus of this book), as this is a measure of social distance and thus consistent with traditional notions of assimilation. However, it is also useful to study the *locational attainment* of immigrants. This term refers to the quality of neighborhoods in which people reside. Understanding neighborhood quality can provide information about whether immigrants (and their children) are experiencing unequal residential outcomes compared to the native-born population. Residential segregation and locational attainment do not always perfectly correlate. There are many examples of some high-status immigrant communities with good schools and low crime that are also ethnically homogeneous. Understanding patterns of both residential segregation and locational attainment would provide complementary pieces of information about immigrant adaptation and incorporation in the United States.

In conclusion, immigration has dramatically transformed America's neighborhoods, and it will continue to do so for the foreseeable future. Such change inevitably provokes anxiety among many people who have a stake in the maintenance of their communities. Evidence provided in this book, while pointing to a still uncertain future, suggests that America's metropolitan areas are *not* irrevocably splintering into hostile and homogeneous ethnically based neighborhoods as never before. Certainly, ethnic-group affiliations continue to play important and frequently positive and vital roles in the organization of American life. Nevertheless, there are also a growing number of places where many groups share residential space, and in these places these groups are often creating new kinds of connections and new kinds of communities.

METHODS OF MEASURING SEGREGATION AND METHODOLOGICAL DETAILS OF ANALYSES

METHODOLOGICAL ISSUES

Residential segregation has been studied with a variety of measures. The main methodological issues confronting researchers analyzing racial and ethnic segregation revolve around the definition of racial and ethnic categories, geographic areas, and segregation measures.

Race and Ethnicity

The way in which racial and ethnic groups have been defined has changed over time, as race is generally considered to be largely socially constructed rather than biologically based. Residential segregation indexes in the United States generally rely on official government definitions of racial and ethnic groups, given that the data needed to calculate indexes come from the U.S. decennial census. Censuses contain the detailed geographic population counts at the neighborhood level that permit the calculation of common segregation measures. In the first decennial census in 1790, information was collected about whites and blacks only. Over time, data on other groups were collected, often reflecting changing social views of race. In the 2000 census there were essentially five race categories: white, black, American Indian and Alaska Native, Asian, and native Hawaiian or other Pacific Islander. Individuals could also identify themselves as more than one race, in contrast to previous censuses.

Hispanic origin was dealt with in a separate question, and it was sometimes referred to as an "ethnicity" rather than a race.

In practice, the minority groups most studied in the United States today are African Americans, Hispanics, and Asians. Examining the segregation of the American Indian population, and particularly trends over time, is challenging due to the relatively small population of this group as well as changing patterns of self-identification among American Indians.[1]

Geographic Areas

Residential segregation typically (though not always) describes the distribution of different groups across smaller areal units within larger areas. Thus, to measure residential segregation, one usually has to define both the appropriate larger area and its component parts. The most common larger geographic unit chosen is the metropolitan area, which is a reasonable approximation of a housing market. Using housing markets as a geographic area is based on the notion that a person (or family) who works in a given area can potentially choose to live in any community within the housing market. In the United States, metropolitan areas generally contain at least 50,000 people, and in 2000 there were 331 of them. The smaller unit chosen is usually the census tract, which was originally designed by the U.S. Census Bureau to represent neighborhoods. Tracts typically have between 2,500 and 8,000 people, with an average of about 4,000. Some researchers have used smaller component units, such as *blocks* or *block groups.* Using smaller component units tends to yield higher segregation scores, as smaller units tend to be racially more homogeneous than larger ones—though the correlation between the smaller and larger areal measures is high.

Segregation Measures

The two most common measures of segregation are the dissimilarity and isolation indexes. The *dissimilarity index* is a measure of evenness, and it ranges from 0 (complete integration) to 1 (complete segregation). It describes the proportion of a group's population that would have to change residence for each neighborhood to have the same racial/ethnic distribution as the metropolitan area overall. The *isolation index* is a measure of exposure and also ranges from 0 to 1, with 1 indicating the highest level of isolation. It indicates the average percentage of minority group members (of the minority group of interest) in the neighborhood where the typical minority group individual lives.

Many other segregation measures have been developed and used by researchers. In 1988, Douglas Massey and Nancy Denton compiled twenty existing measures and identified five dimensions of residential segregation: evenness, exposure, concentration, centralization, and clustering.

Evenness describes the differential distribution of subgroups of the population across neighborhoods. *Exposure* measures potential contact between groups. *Concentration* refers to the relative amount of physical space occupied by a group. *Centralization* indicates the degree to which a group is located near the center of an urban area. *Clustering* measures the degree to which group members live in contiguous areas.

The measurement of the spatial patterning of the urban populations in U.S. cities has continued to evolve. There is increasing focus upon multiple, complementary measures. Along these lines, there is increasing interest in *spatial* measures of segregation. The most commonly used measures of segregation—dissimilarity and isolation—are "aspatial" in that they do not account for the spatial relationships among census tracts.[2] That is, while dissimilarity and isolation measure the distribution of the population across census tracts (or smaller units, such as blocks), they do not use information on whether particular tracts (or blocks) are in close proximity to each other. At least one recent study has suggested that there are two primary conceptual dimensions to spatial segregation rather than five: spatial exposure and spatial evenness.[3] One drawback of spatial measures of segregation is that they are more complicated to calculate than dissimilarity and isolation. However, with increasing computational power available to researchers, along with advances in GIS software, it will likely become easier to calculate spatial segregation measures in the future.

Another important methodological issue revolves around whom to use as the "reference group" in segregation calculations. The traditional dissimilarity and isolation indexes compare the residential patterns of only two groups at a time. In the United States, studies have typically measured the segregation of various groups from non-Hispanic whites. Researchers increasingly support calculating additional indexes (perhaps supplementing traditional indexes) for all groups with alternative reference groups, such as all people not in the group of interest. For example, segregation indexes could be calculated for non-Hispanic whites vis-à-vis all others, non-Hispanic blacks vis-à-vis all others, and so forth, for all groups. Researchers sometimes also examine the segregation of two minority groups from each other, such as the segregation of African Americans from Hispanics.

Along these lines, there is growing interest in *multigroup* segregation measures that allow researchers to consider multiple racial and ethnic groups, multiple geographic levels (e.g., metropolitan area or regions), or multiple characteristics (race, class, age) simultaneously.[4] Especially with the growing diversity of the population in many countries—in the wake of increasing immigration over the past few decades—it is likely that multigroup measures will become more popular in the coming years.

Finally, there will likely be growing interest in other measures of "integration" or "diversity" calculated at the neighborhood and/or metropolitan level. While segregation measures typically measure the distribution of groups across neighborhoods within a metropolitan area, diversity measures focus on the composition of smaller areal units (such as census tracts), perhaps summarizing this information at the metropolitan level. Diversity measures include the *entropy score*, which is calculated in the derivation of the information theory index, the diversity index, or Simpson's D (or Herfindahl-Hirschman) index.[5] Other possible measures of diversity are possible, such as classifying neighborhoods or metropolitan areas as being multiracial if they meet some sort of compositional criteria[6]—such as having multiple groups present in large numbers—though there is little agreement in the literature of what such criteria should be.

This book relies mainly on three indexes of segregation—dissimilarity, isolation, and information theory (or entropy).[7]

Dissimilarity

As described above, the dissimilarity index is a measure of evenness. It is computed as:

$$D = .5 * \sum_{i=1}^{n} |x_i/X - y_i/Y| \qquad (A.1)$$

where n is the number of tracts in a metropolitan area, x_i is the population size of the minority group of interest in tract i, X is the population of the minority group in the metropolitan area as a whole, y_i is the population of the reference group (usually non-Hispanic whites) in tract i, and Y is the population of the reference group in the metropolitan area as a whole.

Isolation

The isolation index is a measure of exposure. It is computed as:

$$_xP^*_x = \sum_{i=1}^{n} \left[(x_i/X)(x_i/t_i) \right] \tag{A.2}$$

where $_xP^*_x$ is the usual notation for the isolation index, x_i is the population size of the minority group of interest in tract i, X is the population of the minority group in the metropolitan area as a whole, and t_i refers to the sum of the minority and reference group populations in tract i.

Entropy Score and Information Theory (Entropy) Index

An entropy score is a measure of diversity, and the information theory index (sometimes referred to as the entropy index, or Theil's H) measures the distribution of groups across neighborhoods. The entropy score is used in the calculation of the information theory index. First, a metropolitan area's entropy score is calculated as:

$$E = \sum_{r=1}^{r} (\Pi_r) \ln[1/\Pi_r] \tag{A.3}$$

where Π_r refers to a particular racial/ethnic group's proportion of the whole metropolitan area population. All logarithmic calculations use the natural log.[8]

Unlike the information theory index, this formula describes the *diversity* in a metropolitan area. The higher the number, the more diverse an area is. The maximum level of entropy is given by the natural log of the number of groups used in the calculations.

In the empirical analysis in this book, six mutually exclusive and exhaustive categories were constructed: non-Hispanic whites, non-Hispanic African Americans, non-Hispanic Asians and Pacific Islanders, non-Hispanic American Indians and Alaska Natives, non-Hispanics of other races, and Hispanics. Having mutually exclusive and exhaustive categories is essential for constructing a single multiracial index. With six racial/ethnic groups, the maximum entropy is log 6, or 1.792. The maximum score occurs when all groups have equal representation in the geographic area, such that with six groups, for example, each would make up about 17 percent of the area's population. This is not a segregation measure per se because it does not measure the distribution of these groups across a metropolitan area. A metropolitan area, for example, can be very diverse if all minority groups are present, but also highly segregated if all groups live exclusively in their own neighborhoods.

A unit within the metropolitan area, such as a census tract, would analogously have its entropy score, or diversity, defined as

$$E_i = \sum_{r=1}^{r} (\Pi_{ri}) \ln[1/\Pi_{ri}] \qquad (A.4)$$

where Π_{ri} refers to a particular racial/ethnic group's proportion of the population in tract i.

The information theory index is the weighted average deviation of each unit's entropy from the metropolitan-wide entropy, expressed as a fraction of the metropolitan area's total entropy:

$$H = \sum_{i=1}^{n} \left[\frac{t_i(E-E_i)}{ET} \right] \qquad (A.5)$$

where t_i refers to the total population of tract i, T is the metropolitan area population, n is the number of tracts, and E_i and E represent tract i's diversity (entropy) and metropolitan area diversity, respectively. The information theory index varies between 0, when all areas have the same composition as the entire metropolitan area (i.e., maximum integration), to a high of 1, when all areas contain one group only (i.e., maximum segregation). While the entropy score is influenced by the relative size of the various groups in a metropolitan area, the information theory index, being a measure of evenness, is not. Rather, it measures how evenly groups are distributed across metropolitan area neighborhoods, regardless of the size of each of the groups.

DATA AND METHODS FOR
THE ANALYSIS IN CHAPTER 4

The data for the analysis in chapter 4 were drawn from restricted 1990 and 2000 census long-form files. Access to the census data was obtained through an agreement with the U.S. Census Bureau.[9] While residential segregation can occur at any geographic level, I focus on metropolitan areas as reasonable approximations of housing markets. I present estimates for all metropolitan statistical areas (MSAs), primary metropolitan statistical areas (PMSAs), and, for New England states, New England county metropolitan areas (NECMAs), all together referred to hereafter as metropolitan areas (MAs). When comparable data for 1990 and 2000 were presented, the 2000 boundaries of county-based metropolitan areas, as defined by the Office of Management and Budget (OMB) on June 30, 1999, were used to ensure comparability. Segregation indexes were computed for groups that had at least 100,000 members in the United States and at least 1,000 in a particular metropolitan area, because segregation indexes for small minority populations are less reliable than those for larger ones.[10]

To examine the distribution of different groups across neighborhoods within metropolitan areas, I used census tracts. Census tracts typically have between 2,500 and 8,000 individuals, are defined with local input, are intended to represent neighborhoods, and typically do not change much from census to census, except to subdivide. In addition, census tracts are by far the unit most used in research on residential segregation. Thus, the data include information on population counts for all racial groups and for Hispanics by census tract in all metropolitan areas, as well as counts of these groups by nativity and, among the foreign-born, year of entry. I excluded counts of individuals in institutional group quarters (such as prisons).

The 1990 census collected information on four race groups: white; black; American Indian, Eskimo, or Aleut; and Asian or Pacific Islander. There was an additional question on whether an individual was of Hispanic origin. In the 1990s, after much research and public comment, OMB revised the racial classification for the 2000 census to include five categories—white, black or African American, American Indian or Alaska Native, Asian, and native Hawaiian or other Pacific Islander—and allowed individuals to report more than one race. Chapter 4 focuses on the residential patterns of blacks, Hispanics, and Asians, as well as non-Hispanic white immigrants in some analyses (non-Hispanic whites are included in the analyses that focus on the foreign-born only, as native-born non-Hispanic whites are the reference group in the segregation calculations). For 2000, minority groups in this analysis include those who identified as being a member of that minority group either alone or in combination with another race. Non-Hispanic whites consist of those who marked only white and who indicated that they were not Hispanic. The reference group in the segregation calculations is native-born non-Hispanic whites.[11]

Multivariate Analysis

For the multivariate analysis results, the model estimated is described by the following:

$$Y_{ji} = B_0 + B_1 X_{ji} + B_2 Z_j + e_{ji} \tag{A.6}$$

where Y_{ji} is the dissimilarity score for metropolitan area j and group of interest i for each metropolitan area with at least 1,000 group i members present, X_{ji} is a vector of group i characteristics in metropolitan area j, and Z_j is a vector of metropolitan characteristics for metropolitan area j, and B_0, B_1, and B_2 are regression coefficients. The unit of analysis is the metropolitan area, though models include multiple observations per metropolitan area that contain information on the different nativity or year-of-entry groups, depending on the model. The reference group for all the segregation calculations (Y_{ji}) is native-born non-Hispanic whites. Separate models were run for blacks, Hispanics, and Asians.

This approach essentially follows Massey and Denton's strategy of pooling group metropolitan dissimilarity scores and including dummy variables for each group comparison.[12] For example, in the examination of Hispanic patterns of segregation by nativity, each metropolitan area contributes up to two observations: one indicates the dissimilarity index for native-born Hispanics and the other the dissimilarity index for foreign-born Hispanics.[13] A dummy variable for nativity will indicate whether dissimilarity scores are higher for the foreign-born or native-born.

In a second group of models, I examined year-of-entry groups among foreign-born blacks, Hispanics, Asians, and whites. I again stratified models by race and ethnicity. Four year-of-entry categories were used: 0–10 years ago, 11–20 years ago, 21–30 years ago, and 31+ years ago. Thus, in these regressions, there are up to four observations per metropolitan area. Because the same metropolitan areas were included several times in all of the models, corrected standard errors were produced by using generalized linear regression models that account for the correlated error structure among the independent variables.

The *X*-vector variables in the regression models represent group i characteristics in metropolitan area j in each metropolitan area. The variables include group size, English-language proficiency (percentage who speak English very well or well), median household income, and housing tenure (percentage owning homes).[14] It should be noted that these models are not strictly causal, as segregation can affect groups' levels of socioeconomic attainment and English-language proficiency. Rather, the goal is to examine the relationship between segregation and these group characteristics, and how these characteristics might help explain the broader association between nativity and segregation.

Z is a vector of metropolitan area characteristics that have been shown to be associated with segregation.[15] This includes metropolitan area size, percentage of the population that is minority, percentage of the civilian labor force that is in manufacturing and government, percentage of the labor force that is in the military, percentage of the population that is over sixty-five years old, proportion of the population eighteen or older that is enrolled in school, percentage of housing units built in the past ten years, percentage of the metropolitan area population in the suburbs, and region.

All of the regression models are unweighted. The models do, however, include controls for both the size of the group in question (an X_{ji} variable) and the log of the total metropolitan population size (a Z_j variable). I present findings of the relationship between these variables and dissimilarity in 2000. I also ran other models where the dependent variable represented changes in segregation for group of interest i and metropolitan area j between 1990 and 2000 but do not present these results because they show patterns similar to the cross-sectional models.

DATA AND METHODS
FOR THE ANALYSIS IN CHAPTER 5

The analysis in chapter 5 relies on the same restricted-use data from the 2000 census as was used in chapter 4. The analysis in chapter 5 compares levels of residential segregation between several Hispanic subgroups and native-born Anglos, native-born African Americans, and native-born Hispanics of a different race from the group in question in all metropolitan areas where the groups are present in sufficient numbers. As in chapter 4, dissimilarity indexes were computed for groups that have at least 100,000 members in the United States and at least 1,000 in a particular metropolitan area.

Respondent race and Hispanic ethnicity were determined by two questions on the 2000 census. The first question asks, "Is this person Spanish/Hispanic/Latino?" There is an answer box for "no," and then additional "yes" boxes where people also indicate if they are Mexican, Puerto Rican, or Cuban. There is also a write-in box where respondents can identify other origins. The next question on the census form asks, "What is this person's race?" There are answer boxes for white, black, and American Indian or Alaska Native, and a series of boxes for various Asian groups (e.g., Chinese, Filipino, Japanese). People can also mark "some other race" and, unlike in previous censuses, respondents are instructed that they can choose more than one race.

This analysis focuses on the residential patterns of those who reported that they were Hispanic in the first question mentioned above. I look at differences in residential patterns of Hispanics also by whether they indicated their race to be white alone, black alone, or some other race or any combination of races. People are classified as non-Hispanic white (Anglo) or non-Hispanic black (African American) if they marked only those boxes alone and also reported being not Hispanic.

When I look at the segregation of foreign-born Hispanics by country of origin, I use data directly from the question asking, "Where was this person born?" There are two answer boxes, one box for "in the United States," where people are asked to print the name of the state, and a second box for "outside of the United States," where people are asked to print the name of the foreign country, or Puerto Rico, Guam, and so on. As conventionally done in studies of the foreign-born, the foreign-born population in this analysis includes people who reported that they were born outside of the United States and who are either not citizens or U.S. citizens by naturalization (this excludes U.S. citizens who were born abroad of American parents). Hispanic individuals born in Puerto Rico or other outlying territories of the United States, although U.S. citizens at birth, are coded as "foreign-born" in this chapter based on their shared experiences as newcomers to the mainland United States. That is, according to the spatial assimilation model, it is reasonable to hypothesize that migrants from Puerto Rico would be more segregated from whites than Puerto Ricans born within mainland states.

While the analysis in chapter 5 relies on the use of the dissimilarity index, I also conducted analyses with the isolation index. Due to the length and breadth of the current study, I limited the discussion to dissimilarity. The conclusions do not change much with use of the isolation index.[16]

The chapter 5 analysis begins with a descriptive look at dissimilarity scores by race, nativity, and country of origin. In particular, I examine the segregation of white, black, and other-race Hispanics, by nativity, from U.S.-born non-Hispanic whites (Anglos), U.S.-born non-Hispanic blacks (African Americans), and U.S.-born Hispanics not of one's own race. The purpose here is to get a broad sense of what patterns of spatial assimilation we see among various groups of Hispanics.

I use *assimilation* in a precise way: as indicative of the attenuation of group spatial differences across generations. According to assimilation theory, we would expect to see lower Hispanic-Anglo segregation scores among native-born Hispanics than among foreign-born ones, regardless of the race of Hispanic respondents, indicating a pattern of assimilation between first-generation immigrants and U.S.-born generations. Assimilation theory does allow for differences in the level and extent of change across generations among different groups, but we should still witness this type of attenuation for all groups.[17] I compute Hispanic–African American segregation scores to gauge whether Hispanics, and black Hispanics in particular, are more likely to be assimilated by the African American population than by the Anglo population, thus providing some support for segmented assimilation. Finally, I examine Hispanic–"Hispanic not of same race group" segregation to gauge the extent of Hispanic pan-ethnicity spans across self-identified racial groups.[18] In the tables I also show these segregation comparisons by country of origin as the data allow. In particular, I look at the residential patterns of Mexicans, Cubans, and Puerto Ricans by race and nativity to examine the extent of variation by country of origin.

Multivariate Analysis

The statistical model used in chapter 5 is essentially the same as the one used in chapter 4. The main difference is the use of the different reference groups described above for the segregation calculations. I again ran separate models for white Hispanics, black Hispanics, and other-race Hispanics.

The X-vector variables in the regression models that represent group i characteristics in metropolitan area j include group size, English-language proficiency (percentage who speak English very well or well), country of origin (Mexico, Cuba, Puerto Rico, or other), median household income relative to the reference group, and housing tenure (percentage owning homes).[19] The Z-vector variables that represent metropolitan area characteristics include metropolitan area size, percentage of the population that is minority, percentage of the civilian labor force that is in manufacturing and government, percentage of the labor force that is in the military, percentage of the population over sixty-five years old, proportion of the population eighteen or more years old that is enrolled in school, percentage of housing units built in the past ten years, percentage of the metropolitan area population in the suburbs, and region. All of the regression models are again unweighted.

DATA AND METHODS USED IN CHAPTER 6

This analysis in chapter 6 is based on restricted-use Summary File 1 data from the 1980, 1990, and 2000 censuses. Changes in the way race and Hispanic origin data were collected naturally challenge researchers to determine the best way to present historically compatible data. To facilitate comparisons across time, I used minority race/ethnicity definitions that could be closely reproduced in the three different decades and that closely approximate 1990 census categories. I constructed six mutually exclusive and exhaustive categories: non-Hispanic whites, non-Hispanic African Americans, non-Hispanic Asians and Pacific Islanders, non-Hispanic American Indians and Alaska Natives, non-Hispanics of other races, and Hispanics. Having mutually exclusive and exhaustive categories is essential for constructing a single multiracial index.

For the 2000 census, this involved combining the Asian and Native Hawaiian or other Pacific Islander groups. In addition, non-Hispanic people who identified themselves as being of two or more races in 2000 were also categorized as "other," since people could not mark more than one race in 1980 or 1990. Census 2000 figures indicate that 4.6 million, or 1.6 percent of the population, designated themselves as multiracial (and non-Hispanic). Because of the relatively small number of multiracial people, the impact on segregation of the creation of this category in the 2000 census is small.[20] People who reported being Hispanic were categorized as such, regardless of their response to the race question.

Metropolitan areas (MAs) in this analysis followed boundaries in effect during the 2000 census, issued by the Office of Management and Budget on June 30, 1999. Minor Civil Division–based MSAs and PMSAs were used in New England. In 2000, there were 331 MAs in the United States. For this analysis, six MAs were omitted (Barnstable-Yarmouth, MA, Flagstaff, AZ-UT, Greenville, NC, Jonesboro, AR, Myrtle Beach, SC, and Punta Gorda, FL) because they had fewer than nine census tracts and populations of less than 41,000 in 1980. All other MAs used had populations of at least 50,000 in 1980, which is typically one of the criteria for defining an area as an MA.

Multivariate Analysis

The multivariate analysis linking diversity with segregation was based on reduced-form fixed-effects regressions. The data used in the statistical models contain two observations per metropolitan area, corresponding to changes in metropolitan area characteristics between 1980 and 1990 and 1990 and 2000.[21] The dependent variables in the models are changes in multigroup segregation scores in each of the two decades, and the independent variables likewise represent changes in diversity scores and the decade of change of each observation. The model estimated is described by the following:

$$\Delta H_{ti} = B_0 + B_1(\Delta T 1990_{ti}) + B_2(\Delta D_{ti}) + B_3(\Delta D * \Delta T 1990_{ti}) \quad \text{(A.7)}$$

where i indexes metropolitan areas and t indexes the two decades (1980s and 1990s). $\Delta T 1990$ is a dummy variable with a value of 1 if the observation is for the decade from 1990 to 2000, and 0 if the observation is for the decade from 1980 to 1990. The coefficients can be interpreted as follows: B_0 is the secular trend in H from 1980 to 1990; B_1 is the difference between the 1980 to 1990 secular trend and the 1990 to 2000 secular trend; B_2 is the relationship between changes in diversity and changes in H during the 1980s; and B_3 is the difference in the diversity slope between the 1980s and 1990s.

The analyses contained some variations on this equation, such as the omission of the interaction term (to gauge the gross effect over the 1980 to 2000 period); the models without the interaction term are the ones shown in chapter 6.[22] In other models, the diversity term was replaced by what amounts to its components parts—the change in the percentage of each of the six racial/ethnic groups (the white category is omitted) in the metropolitan area. These permitted a more detailed examination of whether changes in the representation of a particular group were driving the diversity-segregation relationship. Regressions in the chapter 6 analyses are unweighted, though results from unweighted and weighted regressions yield similar results (where the weight is the population size of the metropolitan area).[23]

ADDITIONAL TABLES AND FIGURES

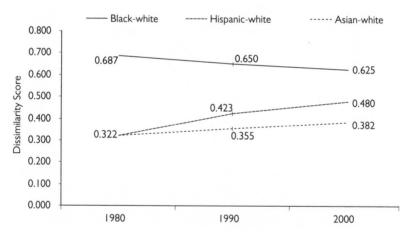

FIGURE B.I. Residential segregation in Washington, D.C., by group: Dissimilarity index, 1980–2000. Source: John Iceland, Daniel H. Weinberg, and Erika Steinmetz (2002), *Racial and Ethnic Residential Segregation in the United States: 1980–2000*, U.S. Census Bureau, Census Special Report, CENSR-3 (Washington, D.C.: U.S. Government Printing Office).

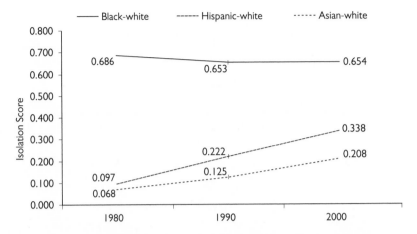

FIGURE B.2. Residential segregation in Washington, D.C., by group: Isolation index, 1980–2000. Source: John Iceland, Daniel H. Weinberg, and Erika Steinmetz (2002), *Racial and Ethnic Residential Segregation in the United States: 1980–2000*, U.S. Census Bureau, Census Special Report, CENSR-3 (Washington, D.C.: U.S. Government Printing Office).

TABLE B.1. Residential Segregation by Race, Hispanic Origin, and Nativity, and Timing of Immigration, 1990 and 2000

	Number of Metropolitan Areas	Dissimilarity Index		Isolation Index	
		1990	*2000*	*1990*	*2000*
All foreign-born people	**187**	**0.411**	**0.443**	**0.402**	**0.474**
1990–2000	187	—	0.517	—	0.375
1980–1989	187	0.514	0.493	0.368	0.341
1970–1979	187	0.462	0.443	0.259	0.238
Before 1970	187	0.302	0.313	0.168	0.153
All Hispanics	**170**	**0.514**	**0.522**	**0.532**	**0.581**
Native-born	170	0.480	0.481	0.435	0.476
Foreign-born	170	0.598	0.599	0.488	0.523
All foreign-born Hispanics	84	0.600	0.602	0.501	0.545
1990–2000	84	—	0.651	—	0.436
1980–1989	84	0.650	0.623	0.434	0.393
1970–1979	84	0.628	0.600	0.344	0.309
Before 1970	84	0.530	0.514	0.279	0.253
All Asians and Pacific Islanders	**157**	**0.434**	**0.434**	**0.291**	**0.341**
Native-born	157	0.402	0.394	0.220	0.232
Foreign-born	157	0.475	0.477	0.233	0.286
All foreign-born Asians and Pacific Islanders	63	0.475	0.482	0.250	0.310
1990–2000	63	—	0.545	—	0.223
1980–1989	63	0.534	0.520	0.215	0.199
1970–1979	63	0.484	0.475	0.115	0.114
Before 1970	63	0.498	0.507	0.084	0.077

	Number of Metropolitan Areas	Dissimilarity Index		Isolation Index	
		1990	*2000*	*1990*	*2000*
All blacks	84	**0.713**	**0.674**	**0.659**	**0.635**
Native-born	84	0.716	0.675	0.654	0.626
Foreign-born	84	0.747	0.712	0.464	0.444
All foreign-born blacks	24	0.754	0.727	0.509	0.508
1990–2000	24	—	0.751	—	0.391
1980–1989	24	0.775	0.751	0.438	0.399
1970–1979	24	0.778	0.754	0.377	0.344
Before 1970	24	0.784	0.772	0.358	0.321
Foreign-born non-Hispanic whites	**91**	**0.271**	**0.305**	**0.116**	**0.142**
1990–2000	91	—	0.470	—	0.113
1980–1989	91	0.451	0.420	0.078	0.053
1970–1979	91	0.408	0.403	0.043	0.034
Before 1970	91	0.247	0.270	0.063	0.046

SOURCE: Analysis of 1990 and 2000 census long-form data.

NOTE: Includes metropolitan areas with at least 1,000 members of the group in question (the weighted total). Weighted means are weighted by the size of the group in question. Higher values indicate more segregation. The reference group is native-born non-Hispanic whites. Number of metropolitan areas is held constant for all year-of-entry categories within each ethnic grouping to facilitate comparison across these categories.

TABLE B.2. Residential Segregation Indexes for Hispanics by Nativity, Country of Origin, and Length of Time in the United States, 2000

	Number of Metropolitan Areas	Dissimilarity Index	Isolation Index
All Hispanics	**317**	**0.477**	**0.568**
Native-born	306	0.475	0.463
Foreign-born	249	0.595	0.513
COUNTRY OF ORIGIN			
Central America	**225**	**0.628**	**0.501**
Mexico	91	0.637	0.513
1995–2000	91	0.690	0.313
1980–1994	91	0.651	0.418
Before 1980	91	0.605	0.354
El Salvador	16	0.713	0.343
1995–2000	16	0.807	0.187
1980–1994	16	0.725	0.299
Before 1980	16	0.720	0.149
Guatemala	12	0.731	0.286
1995–2000	12	0.854	0.186
1980–1994	12	0.758	0.251
Before 1980	12	0.762	0.108
Honduras	6	0.730	0.272
1995–2000	6	0.835	0.187
1980–1994	6	0.759	0.232
Before 1980	6	0.761	0.101
Nicaragua	4	0.619	0.351
1995–2000	4	0.760	0.208
1980–1994	4	0.674	0.331
Before 1980	4	0.678	0.071

	Number of Metropolitan Areas	Dissimilarity Index	Isolation Index
COUNTRY OF ORIGIN			
South America	**95**	**0.538**	**0.228**
Colombia	18	0.584	0.183
1995–2000	18	0.678	0.105
1980–1994	18	0.646	0.124
Before 1980	18	0.595	0.065
Argentina	5	0.559	0.050
1995–2000	5	0.749	0.049
1980–1994	5	0.677	0.029
Before 1980	5	0.671	0.021
Ecuador	10	0.723	0.291
1995–2000	10	0.828	0.204
1980–1994	10	0.777	0.241
Before 1980	10	0.710	0.111
Peru	11	0.608	0.113
1995–2000	11	0.751	0.059
1980–1994	11	0.652	0.085
Before 1980	11	0.070	0.029

SOURCE: Analysis of 2000 census long-form data.

NOTE: Includes metropolitan areas with at least 1,000 members of the group in question. Countries of origin included are those with at least 100,000 emigrants. Weighted means are weighted by the size of the group in question. Higher values indicate more segregation. The reference group is native-born non-Hispanic whites.

TABLE B.3. Residential Segregation Indexes for Asians
and Pacific Islanders by Nativity, Country of Origin,
and Length of Time in the United States, 2000

	Number of Metropolitan Areas	Dissimilarity Index	Isolation Index
All Asians and Pacific Islanders	**299**	**0.398**	**0.329**
Native-born	236	0.392	0.225
Foreign-born	260	0.474	0.276
COUNTRY OF ORIGIN			
Southeast Asia	**187**	**0.550**	**0.234**
Vietnam	28	0.663	0.232
1995–2000	28	0.827	0.108
1980–1994	28	0.711	0.207
Before 1980	28	0.643	0.065
Laos	1	0.763	0.169
1995–2000	1	0.917	0.045
1980–1994	1	0.795	0.153
Before 1980	1	0.787	0.029
Thailand	3	0.700	0.079
1995–2000	3	0.899	0.034
1980–1994	3	0.796	0.079
Before 1980	3	0.780	0.030
Philippines	34	0.572	0.234
1995–2000	34	0.708	0.100
1980–1994	34	0.613	0.177
Before 1980	34	0.590	0.133
Cambodia	1	0.863	0.330
1995–2000	1	0.961	0.076
1980–1994	1	0.886	0.328
Before 1980	1	0.914	0.105

	Number of Metropolitan Areas	Dissimilarity Index	Isolation Index
COUNTRY OF ORIGIN			
East Asia	**166**	**0.525**	**0.220**
Korea	28	0.583	0.158
1995–2000	28	0.757	0.099
1980–1994	28	0.647	0.134
Before 1980	28	0.593	0.049
China	35	0.606	0.266
1995–2000	35	0.712	0.155
1980–1994	35	0.651	0.214
Before 1980	35	0.612	0.122
Japan	12	0.533	0.067
1995–2000	12	0.720	0.042
1980–1994	12	0.645	0.030
Before 1980	12	0.576	0.047
South Central Asia	**126**	**0.570**	**0.117**
India	33	0.576	0.108
1995–2000	33	0.711	0.087
1980–1994	33	0.619	0.067
Before 1980	33	0.642	0.022
Pakistan	5	0.721	0.106
1995–2000	5	0.839	0.074
1980–1994	5	0.756	0.075
Before 1980	5	0.833	0.015

SOURCE: Analysis of 2000 census long-form data.

NOTE: Includes metropolitan areas with at least 1,000 members of the group in question. Countries of origin included are those with at least 100,000 emigrants. Weighted means are weighted by the size of the group in question. Higher values indicate more segregation. The reference group is native-born non-Hispanic whites.

	Number of Metropolitan Areas	Dissimilarity Index	Isolation Index
Ireland	3	0.525	0.047
1995–2000	3	0.839	0.021
1980–1994	3	0.669	0.030
Before 1980	3	0.564	0.024
Western Europe	**152**	**0.332**	**0.021**
France	5	0.561	0.019
1995–2000	5	0.798	0.017
1980–1994	5	0.755	0.012
Before 1980	5	0.659	0.013
Germany	15	0.369	0.018
1995–2000	15	0.763	0.014
1980–1994	15	0.711	0.012
Before 1980	15	0.402	0.014
Southern Europe	**102**	**0.443**	**0.071**
Greece	1	0.688	0.100
1995–2000	1	0.931	0.036
1980–1994	1	0.822	0.034
Before 1980	1	0.698	0.079
Portugal	3	0.671	0.189
1995–2000	3	0.899	0.081
1980–1994	3	0.784	0.154
Before 1980	3	0.639	0.106
Italy	5	0.490	0.062
1995–2000	5	0.840	0.023
1980–1994	5	0.717	0.018
Before 1980	5	0.514	0.057

SOURCE: Analysis of 2000 census long-form data.

NOTE: Includes metropolitan areas with at least 1,000 members of the group in question. Countries of origin included are those with at least 100,000 emigrants. Weighted means are weighted by the size of the group in question. Higher values indicate more segregation. The reference group is native-born non-Hispanic whites.

NOTES

CHAPTER 1

1. U.S. Census Bureau (2000a), "DP-2. Profile of Selected Social Characteristics: 2000," Census 2000 Summary File 3 (SF 3) Sample Data, Census Tract 114, Kings County, New York, available at U.S. Census Bureau, American FactFinder, http://factfinder.census.gov (retrieved July 6, 2007).

2. U.S. Census Bureau (2000c), "QT-P4. Race, Combinations of Two Races, and Not Hispanic or Latino: 2000," Census 2000 Summary File 1 (SF 1) 100-Percent Data; U.S. Census Bureau (2000b), "DP-2. Profile of Selected Social Characteristics: 2000," Census 2000 Summary File 3 (SF 3) Sample Data, Silver Spring, Maryland, both available at U.S. Census Bureau, American FactFinder, http://factfinder.census.gov (retrieved April 1, 2007).

3. Richard D. Alba and Nancy A. Denton (2004), "Old and New Landscapes of Diversity: The Residential Patterns of Immigrant Minorities," in *Not Just Black and White: Historical and Contemporary Perspectives on Immigration, Race, and Ethnicity in the United States*, ed. Nancy Foner and George M. Fredrickson (New York: Russell Sage), 248.

4. U.S. Census Bureau (2003), "Table NST-EST2003-04—Cumulative Estimates of the Components of Population Change for the United States and States: April 1, 2000 to July 1, 2003," U.S. Census Bureau, Population Division, Decem-

5. Daniels (2002, 128–45).

6. Alejandro Portes and Ruben G. Rumbaut (2006), *Immigrant America: A Portrait*, 3rd ed. (Berkeley: University of California Press), 38–40.

7. Daniels (2002, 66–69).

8. Daniels (2002, 136–37, 149–50, 220, 240, 250); Portes and Rumbaut (2006, 39–41).

9. Portes and Rumbaut (2006, 38).

10. Ibid., 62.

11. Ibid., 62; Michael J. White (1987), *American Neighborhoods and Residential Differentiation* (New York: Russell Sage), 97.

12. Douglas S. Massey and Nancy A. Denton (1993), *American Apartheid: Segregation and the Making of the Underclass* (Cambridge: Harvard University Press), 9–10.

13. Robert E. Park (1925), "The City: Suggestions for the Investigation of Human Behavior in the Urban Environment" in *The City*, ed. Robert E. Park and Ernest W. Burgess (Chicago: Chicago University Press), 7.

14. Ibid., 9–10.

15. Robert E. Park and Ernest W. Burgess (1921), *Introduction to the Science of Sociology* (repr., Chicago: University of Chicago Press, 1969), 735.

16. Milton Gordon (1964), *Assimilation in American Life: The Role of Race, Religion, and National Origins* (New York: Oxford University Press), 244.

17. W. E. B. Du Bois (1899), *The Philadelphia Negro: A Social Study* (repr., New York: Schocken Books, 1967), 58.

18. Gunnar Myrdal (1944), *An American Dilemma: The Negro Problem and Modern Democracy* (repr., New Brunswick, NJ: Transaction, 1996), 606–7, 618.

19. Ibid., 620–21.

20. Karl E. Taeuber and Alma F. Taeuber (1965), *Negroes in Cities: Residential Segregation and Neighborhood Change* (Chicago: Aldine), 1–7.

21. Ibid., 2.

22. Stanley Lieberson (1980), *A Piece of the Pie: Blacks and White Immigrants since 1980* (Berkeley: University of California Press), 290–91.

23. Kenneth B. Clark (1965), *Dark Ghetto: Dilemmas of Social Power* (New York: Harper and Row).

24. Massey and Denton (1993, 2).

25. Ibid., 25–26.

26. Ibid., 30–37.

27. Ibid., 84.

28. National Research Council (2006), *Multiple Origins, Uncertain Desti-*

nies: Hispanics and the American Future, ed. Marta Tienda and Faith Mitchell (Washington, D.C.: National Academies Press), 115.

29. Alejandro Portes and Min Zhou (1993), "The New Second Generation: Segmented Assimilation and Its Variants among Post-1965 Immigrant Youth," *Annals of the American Academy of Political and Social Science* 530 (November): 74–96.

30. Alba and Nee (2003, 124–66).

31. Alba and Nee (2003, 11).

32. Portes and Rumbaut (2006, 41); Alba and Nee (2003, 49).

33. Portes and Rumbaut (2006, 41).

34. Alba and Nee (2003, 29).

35. Ibid., 38.

36. Ibid., 255–56.

37. White (1987, 96–98).

38. Daniels (2002, 276).

39. Alba and Nee (2003, 131–32).

40. Daniels (2002, 189, 201–2).

41. Alba and Nee (2003, 126–57).

42. Charles Hirschman, Philip Kasinitz, and Josh DeWind, eds. (1999), *The Handbook of International Migration: The American Experience* (New York: Russell Sage), 129.

43. Bean and Stevens (2003, 98–99).

44. Camille Zubrinsky Charles (2003), "Dynamics of Racial Residential Segregation," *Annual Review of Sociology* 29, 1:167–207; Lawrence Bobo and Camille Zubrinsky (1996), "Attitudes on Residential Integration: Perceived Status Differences, Mere In-Group Preference, or Racial Prejudice?" *Social Forces* 74, 3:883–909; Reynolds Farley, Charlotte Steeh, Maria Krysan, Tara Jackson, and Keith Reeves (1994), "Stereotypes and Segregation: Neighborhoods in the Detroit Area," *American Journal of Sociology* 100, 3:750–80.

45. Camille Zubrinsky Charles (2000), "Neighborhood Racial-Composition Preferences: Evidence from a Multiethnic Metropolis," *Social Problems* 47, 3:370–407. See also Maria Krysan (2002), "Whites Who Say They'd Flee: Who Are They, and Why Would They Leave?" *Demography* 39, 4:675–96.

46. Margery Austin Turner and Stephen L. Ross (2003), *Discrimination in Metropolitan Housing Markets: Phase 2—Asians and Pacific Islanders of the HDS 2000* (Washington, D.C.: U.S. Department of Housing and Urban Development); Margery Austin Turner, Stephen L. Ross, George Galster, and John Yinger (2002), *Discrimination in Metropolitan Housing Markets: National Results*

of Suburban Diversity, Census 2000 Series (Washington, D.C.: Brookings Institution Center on Urban and Metropolitan Policy, June), 1–7; Frey (2006, 1); and Singer (2004, 10).

23. Frey (2001, 7).

24. Audrey Singer (2003), "At Home in the Nation's Capital: Immigrant Trends in Metropolitan Washington" (Washington, D.C.: Brookings Institution Center on Urban and Metropolitan Policy, Greater Washington Research Program, June), 1.

25. U.S. Census Bureau (2006e), "Washington-Arlington-Alexandria, DC-VA-MD-WV Metropolitan Statistical Area Population and Housing Narrative Profile: 2005," American Community Survey data, available at U.S. Census Bureau, American FactFinder, http://factfinder.census.gov (retrieved May 30, 2007).

26. Singer (2003, 4).

27. Douglas S. Massey and Nancy A. Denton (1988), "The Dimensions of Residential Segregation," *Social Forces* 67:281–315.

28. Sean F. Reardon and David O'Sullivan (2004), "Measures of Spatial Segregation," *Sociological Methodology* 34, 1:121–62.

29. John Iceland, Daniel H. Weinberg, and Erika Steinmetz (2002), *Racial and Ethnic Residential Segregation in the United States: 1980–2000*, U.S. Census Bureau, Census Special Report, CENSR-3 (Washington, D.C.: U.S. Government Printing Office).

30. All segregation scores in the figures are weighted by the size of the minority group in question. The scores therefore represent the experience of the average minority group individual.

31. David M. Cutler, Edward L. Glaeser, and Jacob L. Vigdor (1999), "The Rise and Decline of the American Ghetto," *Journal of Political Economy* 107, 3:455–506. See also Douglas S. Massey and Nancy A. Denton (1993), *American Apartheid: Segregation and the Making of the Underclass* (Cambridge: Harvard University Press).

32. Iceland, Weinberg, and Steinmetz (2002, 59–72).

33. Reynolds Farley, Charlotte Steeh, Maria Krysan, Tara Jackson, and Keith Reeves (1994), "Stereotypes and Segregation: Neighborhoods in the Detroit Area," *American Journal of Sociology* 100, 3:750–80.

34. Stephen L. Ross and Margery Austin Turner (2005), "Housing Discrimination in Metropolitan America: Explaining Changes between 1989 and 2000," *Social Problems* 52, 2:152–80.

35. Frey (2006, 6–7).

36. Iceland, Weinberg, and Steinmetz (2002, 64).

37. Mary J. Fischer and Marta Tienda (2006), "Redrawing Spatial Color Lines: Hispanic Metropolitan Dispersal, Segregation, and Economic Opportunity," in *Hispanics and the Future of America*, ed. Marta Tienda and Faith Mitchell (Washington, D.C.: National Academies Press), 110–13.

38. William A.V. Clark (2007), "Race, Class, and Place," *Urban Affairs Review* 42, 3:295–314; Edward L. Glaeser, Matthew E. Kahn, and Jordon Rappaport (2000), "Why Do the Poor Live in Cities?" Discussion Paper Number 1891, Harvard Institute of Economic Research, Cambridge, April.

39. Carmen DeNavas-Walt, Bernadette D. Proctor, and Cheryl Hill Lee (2006), *Income, Poverty, and Health Insurance Coverage in the United States: 2005*, U.S. Census Bureau, Current Population Reports, P60–231 (Washington, D.C.: U.S. Government Printing Office), 5.

40. Peter Fronczek and Patricia Ann Johnson (2003), *Occupations: 2000*, U.S. Census Bureau, Census 2000 Brief, C2KBR-25 (Washington, D.C.: U.S. Government Printing Office), 6; Kurt J. Bauman and Nikki L. Graf (2003), *Educational Attainment: 2000*, U.S. Census Bureau, Census 2000 Brief Series, C2KBR-24 (Washington, D.C.: U.S. Government Printing Office), 5.

41. DeNavas-Walt, Proctor, and Lee (2006, 14).

42. Using the isolation index produces the same general conclusions as using the dissimilarity index, with some exceptions. As mentioned previously, unlike the dissimilarity index, the isolation index is affected by the relative size of the group in question, such that larger groups tend to be more isolated, holding other factors equal, than smaller ones. Results of both indexes when used for most groups indicate that higher-SES groups tend to be less isolated from non-Hispanic whites than low-SES groups, the one exception being that higher-SES Asians are more isolated. Combined with the finding that dissimilarity scores for high-SES Asians are lower than for low-SES Asians, this suggests that the isolation results for Asians are driven in part by the fact that there are relatively more high-SES Asians than low-SES Asians.

43. The findings in figure 5 are also similar if one looks at segregation by education, occupation, or poverty. See John Iceland and Rima Wilkes (2006), "Does Socioeconomic Status Matter? Race, Class, and Residential Segregation," *Social Problems* 52, 2:258.

44. William A.V. Clark and Sarah A. Blue (2004), "Race, Class, and Segregation Patterns in U.S. Immigrant Gateway Cities," *Urban Affairs Review* 39:667–88.

45. See Iceland and Wilkes (2006, 248–73).

the United States as a whole. Using data from the 2000 census, the year-of-entry categories used here are 1995 to 2000, 1980 to 1994, and before 1980. There are fewer categories here than in the previous analysis in order to include a greater number of metropolitan areas where there are at least 1,000 group members in each year-of-entry category. Patterns generally differ a little when ten-year intervals are used (as done in other analyses above), in that segregation for recent arrivals is highest when this category is defined more narrowly, as done in figures 12 through 15. In particular, as would be expected, segregation is higher for "recent" immigrants defined as arriving between 1995 and 2000 than "recent" immigrants defined as arriving between 1990 and 2000.

13. Audrey Singer, Samantha Friedman, Ivan Cheung, and Marie Price (2001), *The World in a Zip Code: Greater Washington, D.C. as a New Region of Immigration* (Washington, D.C.: Brookings Institution Center on Urban and Metropolitan Policy, Greater Washington Research Program, April), 7.

14. Given the relatively small number of African immigrants, these figures show the average levels of segregation for 14 metropolitan areas with more than 1,000 Jamaicans in each of the year-of-entry categories, 8 metropolitan areas with more than 1,000 Haitians in each category, and only 5 metropolitan areas with more than 1,000 Nigerians in each category.

15. Lance Freeman (2002), "Does Spatial Assimilation Work for Black Immigrants in the US?" *Urban Studies* 39, 11:1983–2003.

16. Nancy A. Denton and Douglas S. Massey (1989), "Racial Identity among Caribbean Hispanics: The Effect of Double Minority Status on Residential Segregation," *American Sociological Review* 54 (October): 790–808; Kyle Crowder (1999), "Residential Segregation of West Indians in the New York/New Jersey Metropolitan Area: The Roles of Race and Ethnicity," *International Migration Review* 33, 1:79–113.

17. Crowder (1999, 105).

18. For whites, one potential issue is that scores might be affected by the fact that foreign-born householders in some cases co-reside with their native-born children, and the latter are part of the reference group (native-born non-Hispanic whites). Thus, I also analyzed segregation scores of householders only and found that segregation scores do not differ much.

19. Further analyses (not shown) confirmed that the characteristics of the foreign-born in particular explain their higher levels of segregation rather than characteristics of the metropolitan areas in which they reside.

20. Scott J. South, Kyle Crowder, and Erick Chavez (2005a), "Geographic Mobility and Spatial Assimilation among U.S. Latino Immigrants," *Interna-*

tional Migration Review 39, 3:577–607; Scott J. South, Kyle Crowder, and Erick Chavez (2005b), "Migration and Spatial Assimilation among U.S. Latinos: Classic versus Segmented Trajectories," *Demography* 42, 3:497–521.

21. Audrey Singer (2003), *At Home in the Nation's Capital: Immigrant Trends in Metropolitan Washington* (Washington, D.C.: Brookings Institution Center on Urban and Metropolitan Policy, Greater Washington Research Program, June), 11–13.

22. The simulations are based on multiplying the coefficients shown in table 2 by the ethnic group–specific means of the variables for the native-born population of each ethnic group.

23. It should be noted that the mean indexes differ between table 2 and figure 16. Table 2 shows dissimilarity indexes weighted by the size of the group of interest to show average levels of segregation experienced by group members. In contrast, the multivariate models shown in figure 16 are unweighted because we are interested in variation across metropolitan areas.

24. See, for example, Mary C. Waters (1990), *Ethnic Options: Choosing Identities in America* (Berkeley: University of California Press); and Stanley Lieberson (1980), *A Piece of the Pie: Blacks and White Immigrants since 1980* (Berkeley: University of California Press), 253–91.

25. For more on discrimination, see Stephen L. Ross and Margery Austin Turner (2005), "Housing Discrimination in Metropolitan America: Explaining Changes between 1989 and 2000," *Social Problems* 52, 2:152–80.

26. For more on patterns of economic incorporation among Hispanics, see Frank D. Bean and Gillian Stevens (2003), *America's Newcomers and the Dynamics of Diversity* (New York: Russell Sage).

CHAPTER 5

1. Mary C. Waters (1990), *Ethnic Options: Choosing Identities in America* (Berkeley: University of California Press).

2. Stephen L. Ross and Margery Austin Turner (2005), "Housing Discrimination in Metropolitan America: Explaining Changes between 1989 and 2000," *Social Problems* 52, 2:152–80.

3. Frank D. Bean and Gillian Stevens (2003), *America's Newcomers and the Dynamics of Diversity* (New York: Russell Sage), 114–42; Arthur Sakamoto, Huei-Hsia Wu, and Jessie M. Tzeng (2000), "The Declining Significance of

Identities," in *Not Just Black and White: Historical and Contemporary Perspectives on Immigration, Race, and Ethnicity in the United States*, ed. Nancy Foner and George M. Frederickson (New York: Russell Sage), 212.

26. Philip Rucker and Avis Thomas-Lester (2007), "Shifting Migration Patterns Alter Portrait of Pr. George's," *Washington Post*, July 26, A01.

27. Note that table 4 shows segregation scores for all metropolitan areas where groups meet the population cutoff criteria, such that there are more metropolitan areas in the "All Hispanics" calculation, for example, than in the "Black Hispanics" one. I conducted additional analyses that used only a constant set of metropolitan areas where all groups were present in sufficient numbers. In these analyses, the patterns were similar to those shown in table 4, except that the differences in dissimilarity scores across groups were a little smaller. The scores for the groups in table 4 tend to be a little higher in the restricted (constant) set of metropolitan areas, in part because such metropolitan areas tend to be larger and have higher levels of segregation more generally.

28. Michael E. Martin (2007), *Residential Segregation Patterns of Latinos in the United States, 1990–2000: Testing the Ethnic Enclave and Inequality Theories* (New York: Routledge), 94.

29. Ibid., 95; John R. Logan (2002), *Hispanic Populations and Their Residential Patterns in the Metropolis*, Lewis Mumford Center for Comparative Urban and Regional Research (May 8), http://mumford.albany.edu/census/HispanicPop/HspReportNew/MumfordReport.pdf (retrieved June 21, 2007), 6.

30. Martin (2007, 96–97); Logan (2002, 6).

31. Susan K. Brown (2005), "Delayed Spatial Assimilation: Multi-Generational Incorporation of the Mexican-Origin Population in Los Angeles" (paper presented at the annual meetings of the Population Association of America, Philadelphia, March 31–April 2).

32. The nativity coefficients become insignificant for other-race Hispanics even before metropolitan characteristics are included in the models, according to results not shown in the table.

33. Scott J. South, Kyle Crowder, and Erick Chavez (2005a), "Geographic Mobility and Spatial Assimilation among U.S. Latino Immigrants," *International Migration Review* 39, 3:577–607; Scott J. South, Kyle Crowder, and Erick Chavez (2005b), "Migration and Spatial Assimilation among U.S. Latinos: Classic versus Segmented Trajectories," *Demography* 42, 3:497–521.

34. The coefficients become insignificant in models 2 and 6 in large part because of higher standard errors associated with these coefficients. Nativity

is of course correlated with some of the other variables in the models, such as English-language ability; in models run without the nativity variable, the association between group characteristics did not change significantly except in the case of English-language ability, where associations became stronger between English-language ability and segregation, indicating some collinearity between English-language ability and nativity.

35. Nancy Tejos (2007), "Testing the Boundaries: Latinos Trade Renting in Familiar Enclaves for Owning East of the Anacostia," *Washington Post*, June 9, F01.

36. See William Julius Wilson and Richard P. Taub (2006), *There Goes the Neighborhood* (New York: Alfred A. Knopf), 161–89; Albert M. Camarillio (2004), "Black and Brown in Compton: Demographic Change, Suburban Decline, and Intergroup Relations in a South Central Los Angeles Community, 1950 to 2000," in *Not Just Black and White: Historical and Contemporary Perspectives on Immigration, Race, and Ethnicity in the United States*, ed. Nancy Foner and George M. Frederickson (New York: Russell Sage), 358–76.

37. In other words, the residential patterns of white Hispanics are compared to those of U.S.-born nonwhite Hispanics, black Hispanics are compared to U.S.-born nonblack Hispanics, and other-race Hispanics are compared to U.S.-born white and black Hispanics.

38. Ross and Turner (2005).

39. Michael J. White, Ann H. Him, and Jennifer E. Glick, "Mapping Social Distance: Ethnic Residential Segregation in a Multiethnic Metro," *Sociological Methods and Research* 34, 2 (2005): 173–203.

40. Ross and Turner (2005).

41. Denton and Massey (1989, 805–6).

42. Waters (1994, 816–18).

43. South, Crowder, and Chavez (2005b, 516).

44. Janel E. Benson (2006), "Exploring the Racial Identities of Black Immigrants in the United States," *Sociological Forum* 21, 2:219–47.

45. Kyle Crowder (1999), "Residential Segregation of West Indians in the New York/New Jersey Metropolitan Area: The Roles of Race and Ethnicity," *International Migration Review* 33, 1:107; Waters (1994, 795).

CHAPTER 6

1. Lewis W. Diuguid (2007), "Opinion: Reaching Out to Diversity, One Step at a Time," *Kansas City (MO) Star*, April 4, commentary section.

27. William Julius Wilson and Richard P. Taub (2006), *There Goes the Neighborhood* (New York: Alfred A. Knopf), 161–89.

28. Ellen (2007, 133).

29. John R. Logan and Charles Zhang (2007), "Global Neighborhoods: Pathways to Diversity and Separation" (paper presented at the annual meetings of the Population Association of America, New York, March 29–31, 12.

30. Gabriella Gahlia Modan (2007), *Turf Wars: Discourse, Diversity, and the Politics of Place* (Malden, MA: Blackwell), 9.

31. Richard Florida, *The Rise of the Creative Class: And How It's Transforming Work, Leisure, and Everyday Life* (New York: Basic Books, 2002).

32. Modan (2007, 107).

33. Ibid., 247–65.

34. John R. Logan (2002a), *Choosing Segregation: Racial Imbalance in American Public Schools, 1990–2000*, Lewis Mumford Center for Comparative Urban and Regional Research (March 29), www.s4.brown.edu/cen2000/SchoolPop/SPReport/page1.html (retrieved June 15, 2007), 1.

35. Ellen (2007, 138–39).

36. Robert D. Putnam (2007), "*E Pluribus Unum:* Diversity and Community in the Twenty-first Century; The 2006 Johan Skytte Prize Lecture," *Scandinavian Political Studies* 30, 2:141–42.

37. Ibid., 137.

38. Richard D. Alba and Nancy A. Denton (2004), "Old and New Landscapes of Diversity: The Residential Patterns of Immigrant Minorities," in *Not Just Black and White: Historical and Contemporary Perspectives on Immigration, Race, and Ethnicity in the United States,* ed. Nancy Foner and George M. Frederickson (New York: Russell Sage), 257–58.

39. Nancy Tejos (2007), "Testing the Boundaries: Latinos Trade Renting in Familiar Enclaves for Owning East of the Anacostia," *Washington Post,* June 9, F01.

40. Nestor Rodriguez (1999), "U.S. Immigration and Changing Relations between African Americans and Latinos," in *The Handbook of International Migration,* ed. Charles Hirschman, Philip Kasinitz, and Josh DeWind (New York: Russell Sage), 430.

41. Modan (2007, 120–24).

42. James H. Johnson, Walter C. Farrell Jr., and Chandra Guinn (1999), "Immigration Reform and the Browning of America: Tension, Conflicts, and Community Instability in Metropolitan Los Angeles," in *The Handbook*

of International Migration, ed. Charles Hirschman, Philip Kasinitz, and Josh DeWind (New York: Russell Sage), 399–403.

43. Nancy Foner and George M. Frederickson (2004), introduction in *Not Just Black and White: Historical and Contemporary Perspectives on Immigration, Race, and Ethnicity in the United States,* ed. Nancy Foner and George M. Frederickson (New York: Russell Sage), 13.

44. John Li (2004), "The Black-Asian Conflict?" in *Not Just Black and White: Historical and Contemporary Perspectives on Immigration, Race, and Ethnicity in the United States,* ed. Nancy Foner and George M. Frederickson (New York: Russell Sage), 301–14. See also Steven J. Gold (2004), "Immigrant Entrepreneurs and Customers throughout the Twentieth Century," in *Not Just Black and White: Historical and Contemporary Perspectives on Immigration, Race, and Ethnicity in the United States,* ed. Nancy Foner and George M. Frederickson (New York: Russell Sage), 315–40.

45. Albert M. Camarillio (2004), "Black and Brown in Compton: Demographic Change, Suburban Decline, and Intergroup Relations in a South Central Los Angeles Community, 1950 to 2000," in *Not Just Black and White: Historical and Contemporary Perspectives on Immigration, Race, and Ethnicity in the United States,* ed. Nancy Foner and George M. Frederickson (New York: Russell Sage), 358–76.

46. Maly (2005, 196–201).

47. Barry Edmonston, Sharon M. Lee, and Jeffrey S. Passel (2002), "Recent Trends in Intermarriage and Immigration and Their Effects on the Future Racial Composition of the U.S. Population," in *The New Race Question: How the Census Counts Multiracial Individuals,* ed. Joel Perlmann and Mary C. Waters (New York: Russell Sage), 241.

48. Susan K. Brown (2006), "Structural Assimilation Revisited: Mexican-Origin Nativity and Cross-Ethnic Primary Ties," *Social Forces* 85, 1:75–92.

49. Modan (2007, 238).

50. Putnam (2007, 159–65).

51. Iceland, Weinberg, and Steinmetz (2002, 4); Sharon Lee and Barry Edmonston (2005), "New Marriages, New Families: U.S. Racial and Hispanic Intermarriage," *Population Bulletin* 60, 2:13.

52. U.S. Census Bureau (2006c), "Race," American Community Survey 2005 data, Table B02001, available at U.S. Census Bureau, American Fact-Finder, http://factfinder.census.gov (retrieved June 18, 2007).

53. These dissimilarity scores are unweighted. See William H. Frey and

17. Alejandro Portes and Ruben G. Rumbaut (2006), *Immigrant America: A Portrait*, 3rd ed. (Berkeley: University of California Press), 41.

APPENDIX A

1. See, for example, Gary D. Sandefur, Molly Martin, Jennifer Eggerling-Boeck, Susan E. Mannon, and Ann M. Meier (2001), "An Overview of Racial and Ethnic Demographic Trends," in *America Becoming: Racial Trends and Their Consequences*, vol. 1, ed. Neil J. Smelser, William Julius Wilson, and Faith Mitchell (Washington, D.C.: National Academies Press), 40–102.

2. See Sean F. Reardon and David O'Sullivan (2004), "Measures of Spatial Segregation," *Sociological Methodology* 34, 1:121–62; David S. Wong (1993), "Spatial Indices of Segregation," *Urban Studies* 30:559–72; and Michael J. White (1983), "The Measurement of Spatial Segregation," *American Journal of Sociology* 88:1008–18.

3. Reardon and Sullivan (2004).

4. See, for example, Sean F. Reardon and Glenn Firebaugh (2002), "Measures of MultiGroup Segregation," *Sociological Methodology* 32, 1:33–67; John Iceland (2004), "Beyond Black and White: Residential Segregation in Multiethnic America," *Social Science Research* 33, 2 (June): 248–71; Claude S. Fischer, Gretchen Stockmayer, Jon Stiles, and Michael Hout (2004), "Geographic Levels and Social Dimensions of Metropolitan Segregation," *Demography* 41:37–60; and Mary J. Fischer (2003), "The Relative Importance of Income and Race in Determining Residential Outcomes in U.S. Urban Areas, 1970–2000," *Urban Affairs Review* 38, 5:669–96.

5. The information theory index is described in Henry Theil (1972), *Statistical Decomposition Theory* (New York: American Elsevier); and Reardon and Firebaugh (2002). The diversity index is described in Michael T. Maly (2000), "The Neighborhood Diversity Index," *Journal of Urban Affairs* 22, 1:37–47. For a description of all of these measures, see also U.S. Census Bureau (2005a), *Peer Review of "Racial and Ethnic Residential Segregation in the United States: 1980–2000,"* U.S. Census Bureau (January), www.census.gov/hhes/www/housing/resseg/peer_review.html (retrieved July 3, 2007).

6. See Ingrid Gould Ellen (2007), "How Integrated Did We Become during the 1990s?" in *Fragile Rights within Cities: Government, Housing, and Fairness*, ed. John Goering (Lanham, MD: Rowman and Littlefield, 2007), 123; and David Fasenfest, Jason Booza, and Kurt Metzger (2004), *Living Together: A New Look at Racial and Ethnic Integration in Metropolitan Neighborhoods, 1990–2000*, Living

Cities Census Series (Washington, D.C.: Brookings Institution Center on Urban and Metropolitan Policy, April), available at www.brookings.edu/reports/2004/04demographics_fasenfest.aspx (retrieved June 15, 2007).

7. For an illustration of the five dimensions of segregation, and the formulas of nineteen measures used in a U.S. Census Bureau segregation report, see John Iceland, Daniel H. Weinberg, and Erika Steinmetz (2002), *Racial and Ethnic Residential Segregation in the United States: 1980–2000*, U.S. Census Bureau, Census Special Report, CENSR-3 (Washington, D.C.: U.S. Government Printing Office), 9–13, 119–23.

8. When the proportion of a particular group in a given census tract (Π_r) is 0, then the log is set to 0. This is the preferred procedure, as the absence of a group (or multiple groups) should result in a 0 increase in the entropy score (where a higher score indicates more diversity).

9. My collaborators and I obtained special sworn status from the Census Bureau and approval from the Census Internal Review Board to use the data.

10. Random factors and geocoding errors are more likely to play a large role in determining the settlement pattern of group members when fewer members are present, causing these indexes to contain greater volatility. See, for example, Iceland, Weinberg, and Steinmetz (2002, 13–14); and Douglas S. Massey and Nancy A. Denton (1988), "The Dimensions of Residential Segregation," *Social Forces* 67:281–315.

11. My more inclusive racial definitions mean that the minority group definitions are not mutually exclusive. Some of those who are black may also, for example, be Asian. Other work has shown that adopting a race definition where a person is considered in a group if he or she chooses only that particular group has little effect on African American segregation calculations and a modest effect on Asian segregation calculations. See Iceland, Weinberg, and Steinmetz (2002, 117–18). The similarity of scores across group definitions results, in large part, from the fact that the proportion of people who marked two or more race groups in the 2000 census was small (2.4 percent). Hispanic indexes are not affected by this specific issue, since Hispanic origin is asked about in a separate question. Methodologically, the most important issue is to ensure that the two groups used in any given index calculation are mutually exclusive, which is indeed the case in this analysis.

12. Douglas S. Massey and Nancy A. Denton (1989), "Hypersegregation in U.S. Metropolitan Areas: Black and Hispanic Segregation along Five Dimensions," *Demography* 26:373–93.

REFERENCES

Adelman, Robert M., Hui-shien Tsao, Stewart E. Tolnay, and Kyle D. Crowder. 2001. "Neighborhood Disadvantage among Racial and Ethnic Groups: Residential Location in 1970 and 1980." *Sociological Quarterly* 42, 4:603–32.

Aizenman, N.C. 2007. "Small-Town Resistance Helped to Seal Defeat." *Washington Post*, June 29, A01.

Alba, Richard D., and Nancy A. Denton. 2004. "Old and New Landscapes of Diversity: The Residential Patterns of Immigrant Minorities." In *Not Just Black and White: Historical and Contemporary Perspectives on Immigration, Race, and Ethnicity in the United States*, edited by Nancy Foner and George M. Frederickson, 237–61. New York: Russell Sage.

Alba, Richard D., and Victor Nee. 2003. *Remaking the American Mainstream: Assimilation and Contemporary Immigration*. Cambridge: Harvard University Press.

Bailey, Raleigh. 2005. "New Immigrant Communities in the North Carolina Piedmont Triad: Integration Issues and Challenges." In *Beyond the Gateway: Immigrants in a Changing America*, edited by Elżbieta M. Goździak and Susan F. Martin, 57–85. Lanham: Lexington Books.

Batson, Christie D., Zhenchao Qian, and Daniel T. Lichter. 2006. "Interracial and Intraracial Patterns of Mate Selection among America's Diverse Black Populations." *Journal of Marriage and Family* 68 (August): 658–72.

Bauman, Kurt J., and Nikki L. Graf. 2003. *Educational Attainment: 2000*. U.S. Census Bureau, Census 2000 Brief Series, C2KBR-24. Washington, D.C.: U.S. Government Printing Office.

Bean, Frank D., Jennifer Lee, Jeanne Batalova, and Mark Leach. 2004. *The American People: Immigration and Fading Color Lines in America*. Census 2000 Report. New York: Russell Sage.

Bean, Frank D., and Gillian Stevens. 2003. *America's Newcomers and the Dynamics of Diversity*. New York: Russell Sage.

Benson, Janel E. 2006. "Exploring the Racial Identities of Black Immigrants in the United States." *Sociological Forum* 21, 2 (June): 219–47.

Bobo, Lawrence, and Camille Zubrinsky. 1996. "Attitudes on Residential Integration: Perceived Status Differences, Mere In-Group Preference, or Racial Prejudice?" *Social Forces* 74, 3:883–909.

Brodsky, Alyn B. 2000. *Grover Cleveland: A Study in Character*. New York: Truman Talley Books.

Brown, Susan K. 2005. "Delayed Spatial Assimilation: Multi-Generational Incorporation of the Mexican-Origin Population in Los Angeles." Paper presented at the annual meetings of the Population Association of America, Philadelphia, March 31–April 2.

———. 2006. "Structural Assimilation Revisited: Mexican-Origin Nativity and Cross-Ethnic Primary Ties." *Social Forces* 85, 1:75–92.

Camarillo, Albert M. 2004. "Black and Brown in Compton: Demographic Change, Suburban Decline, and Intergroup Relations in a South Central Los Angeles Community, 1950 to 2000." In *Not Just Black and White: Historical and Contemporary Perspectives on Immigration, Race, and Ethnicity in the United States*, edited by Nancy Foner and George M. Frederickson, 358–76. New York: Russell Sage.

Charles, Camille Zubrinsky. 2000. "Neighborhood Racial-Composition Preferences: Evidence from a Multiethnic Metropolis." *Social Problems* 47, 3:370–407.

———. 2003. "Dynamics of Racial Residential Segregation." *Annual Review of Sociology* 29, 1:167–207.

———. 2005. "Can We Live Together?" In *The Geography of Opportunity*, edited by Xavier de Souza Briggs. Washington, D.C.: Brookings Institution Press.

———. 2006. *Won't You Be My Neighbor? Race, Class, and Residence in Los Angeles*. New York: Russell Sage.

Charles, Camille Zubrinsky, Gniesha Dinwiddie, and Douglas S. Massey. 2004.

"The Continuing Consequences of Segregation: Family Stress and College Academic Performance." *Social Science Quarterly* 85, 5:1353–73.

Clark, Kenneth B. 1965. *Dark Ghetto: Dilemmas of Social Power*. New York: Harper and Row.

Clark, William A. V. 2007. "Race, Class, and Place." *Urban Affairs Review* 42, 3:295–314.

Clark, William A. V., and Sarah A. Blue. 2004. "Race, Class, and Segregation Patterns in U.S. Immigrant Gateway Cities." *Urban Affairs Review* 39, 6:667–88.

Cohn, D'Vera. 2002. "Integrated People, Integrated Places; Multirace Residents Pick Neighborhoods of Diversity." *Washington Post*, July 29, B01.

Cornell, Stephen, and Douglas Hartmann. 2004. "Conceptual Confusions and Divides: Race, Ethnicity, and the Study of Immigration." In *Not Just Black and White: Historical and Contemporary Perspectives on Immigration, Race, and Ethnicity in the United States*, edited by Nancy Foner and George M. Frederickson, 23–41. New York: Russell Sage.

Crèvecoeur, J. Hector St. John. 1782. *Letters from an American Farmer*. Reprint, New York: Albert and Charles Boni, 1925.

Crowder, Kyle. 1999. "Residential Segregation of West Indians in the New York/New Jersey Metropolitan Area: The Roles of Race and Ethnicity." *International Migration Review* 33, 1:79–113.

Cutler, David M., and Edward L. Glaeser. 1997. "Are Ghettos Good or Bad?" *The Quarterly Journal of Economics* 112, 3:827–72.

Cutler, David M., Edward L. Glaeser, and Jacob L. Vigdor. 1999. "The Rise and Decline of the American Ghetto." *Journal of Political Economy* 107, 3: 455–506.

Daniels, Roger. 2002. *Coming to America*. 2nd ed. New York: Perennial.

DeNavas-Walt, Carmen, Bernadette D. Proctor, and Cheryl Hill Lee. 2006. *Income, Poverty, and Health Insurance Coverage in the United States: 2005*. U.S. Census Bureau, Current Population Reports, P60–231. Washington, D.C.: U.S. Government Printing Office.

Denton, Nancy A., and Douglas S. Massey. 1989. "Racial Identity among Caribbean Hispanics: The Effect of Double Minority Status on Residential Segregation." *American Sociological Review* 54:790–808.

———. 1991. "Patterns of Neighborhood Transition in a Multi-Ethnic World: U.S. Metropolitan Areas, 1970–1980." *Demography* 28, 1:41–63.

Diuguid, Lewis W. 2007. "Opinion: Reaching Out to Diversity, One Step at a Time." *Kansas City (MO) Star*, April 4, commentary section.

Du Bois, W.E.B. 1899. *The Philadelphia Negro: A Social Study*. Reprint, New York: Schocken Books, 1967.

———. 1903. *The Souls of Black Folk*. Reprint, New York: Signet Classic, 1995.

Duncan, Otis Dudley, and Beverly Duncan. 1968. *The Negro Population of Chicago: A Study of Residential Succession*. Chicago: University of Chicago Press.

Edmonston, Barry, Sharon M. Lee, and Jeffrey S. Passel. 2002. "Recent Trends in Intermarriage and Immigration and Their Effects on the Future Racial Composition of the U.S. Population." In *The New Race Question: How the Census Counts Multiracial Individuals*, edited by Joel Perlmann and Mary C. Waters. New York: Russell Sage.

Ellen, Ingrid Gould. 2000. *Sharing America's Neighborhoods: The Changing Prospects for Stable Racial Integration*. Cambridge: Harvard University Press.

———. 2007. "How Integrated Did We Become during the 1990s?" In *Fragile Rights within Cities: Government, Housing, and Fairness*, edited by John Goering. Lanham, MD: Rowman and Littlefield.

Farley, Reynolds, and William H. Frey. 1994. "Changes in the Segregation of Whites from Blacks during the 1980s: Small Steps toward a More Integrated Society." *American Sociological Review* 59:23–45.

Farley, Reynolds, Charlotte Steeh, Maria Krysan, Tara Jackson, and Keith Reeves. 1994. "Stereotypes and Segregation: Neighborhoods in the Detroit Area." *American Journal of Sociology* 100, 3:750–80.

Fasenfest, David, Jason Booza, and Kurt Metzger. 2004. *Living Together: A New Look at Racial and Ethnic Integration in Metropolitan Neighborhoods, 1990–2000*. Living Cities Census Series. Washington, D.C.: Brookings Institution Center on Urban and Metropolitan Policy, April. Available at www.brookings .edu/reports/2004/04demographics_fasenfest.aspx (retrieved June 15, 2007).

Fischer, Claude S., and Michael Hout. 2006. *Century of Difference: How America Changed in the Last One Hundred Years*. New York: Russell Sage.

Fischer, Claude S., Gretchen Stockmayer, Jon Stiles, and Michael Hout. 2004. "Geographic Levels and Social Dimensions of Metropolitan Segregation." *Demography* 41, 1:37–60.

Fischer, Mary J. 2003. "The Relative Importance of Income and Race in Determining Residential Outcomes in U.S. Urban Areas, 1970–2000." *Urban Affairs Review* 38, 5:669–96.

Fischer, Mary J., and Marta Tienda. 2006. "Redrawing Spatial Color Lines: Hispanic Metropolitan Dispersal, Segregation, and Economic Opportunity." In *Hispanics and the Future of America*, edited by Marta Tienda and Faith Mitchell, 100–137. Washington, D.C.: National Academies Press.

Florida, Richard. 2002. *The Rise of the Creative Class: And How It's Transforming Work, Leisure, and Everyday Life*. New York: Basic Books.

Foner, Nancy, and George M. Frederickson. 2004. Introduction in *Not Just Black and White: Historical and Contemporary Perspectives on Immigration, Race, and Ethnicity in the United States*, edited by Nancy Foner and George M. Frederickson, 1–19. New York: Russell Sage.

Freeman, Lance. 2002. "Does Spatial Assimilation Work for Black Immigrants in the US?" *Urban Studies* 39, 11:1983–2003.

Frey, William H. 2001a. *Melting Pot Suburbs: A Census 2000 Study of Suburban Diversity*. Census 2000 Series. Washington, D.C.: Brookings Institution Center on Urban and Metropolitan Policy, June.

———. 2001b. "Segregation: Neighborhood Exposure by Race." Data available at CensusScope, www.censusscope.org (retrieved June 19, 2007).

———. 2006. *Diversity Spreads Out: Metropolitan Shifts in Hispanic, Asian, and Black Populations since 2000*. Living Cities Census Series. Washington, D.C.: Brookings Institution Center on Urban and Metropolitan Policy, March.

Frey, William H., and Reynolds Farley. 1996. "Latino, Asian, and Black Segregation in U.S. Metropolitan Areas: Are Multiethnic Metros Different?" *Demography* 33, 1:35–50.

Frey, William H., and Dowell Myers. 2002. "Neighborhood Segregation in Single-Race and Multirace America: A Census 2000 Study of Cities and Metropolitan Areas." Fannie Mae Foundation Working Paper. www.census scope.org/FreyWPFinal.pdf (retrieved June 18, 2007).

Fronczek, Peter, and Patricia Ann Johnson. 2003. *Occupations: 2000*. U.S. Census Bureau, Census 2000 Brief, C2KBR-25. Washington, D.C.: U.S. Government Printing Office.

Gans, Herbert J. 1999a. "The Possibility of a New Racial Hierarchy in the Twenty-first Century United States." In *The Cultural Territories of Race*, edited by Michele Lamont. Chicago: University of Chicago Press.

———. 1999b. "Toward a Reconciliation of 'Assimilation' and 'Pluralism': The Interplay of Acculturation and Ethnic Retention." In *The Handbook of International Migration: The American Experience*, edited by Charles Hirschman, Philip Kasinitz, and Josh DeWind, 161–71. New York: Russell Sage Foundation.

Gardener, Amy. 2007. "Fairfax Candidate Fights for More Diverse Board." *Washington Post*, March 11, A01.

Gebeloff, Robert, and Mary Jo Patterson. 2006. "The Changing Face of New Jersey." *Newark (NJ) Star Ledger*, December 24, news section, 1.

Glaeser, Edward L., Matthew E. Kahn, and Jordon Rappaport. 2000. "Why Do the Poor Live in Cities?" Discussion Paper Number 1891, Harvard Institute of Economic Research, Cambridge, April.

Goering, John M., and Ron Wienk, eds. 1996. *Mortgage Lending, Racial Discrimination and Federal Policy.* Washington, D.C.: Urban Institute Press.

Gold, Steven J. 2004. "Immigrant Entrepreneurs and Customers throughout the Twentieth Century." In *Not Just Black and White: Historical and Contemporary Perspectives on Immigration, Race, and Ethnicity in the United States,* edited by Nancy Foner and George M. Frederickson, 315–40. New York: Russell Sage.

Gordon, Milton. 1964. *Assimilation in American Life: The Role of Race, Religion, and National Origins.* New York: Oxford University Press.

Grieco, Elizabeth, and Rachel C. Cassidy. 2001. *Overview of Race and Hispanic Origin: 2000.* Census 2000 Brief No. C2KBR/01-1. Washington, D.C.: U.S. Government Printing Office.

Harris, David R., and Hiromi Ono. 2001. *Cohabitation, Marriage and Markets: A New Look at Intimate Interracial Relationships.* Ann Arbor: University of Michigan, Institute for Social Research.

Harris, David R., and Jeremiah Joseph Sim. 2002. "Who Is Multiracial? Assessing the Complexity of Lived Race." *American Sociological Review* 67, 4:614–27.

Harrison, Roderick J., and Claudette Bennett. 1995. "Racial and Ethnic Diversity." In *State of the Union: America in the 1990s,* vol. 2, edited by Reynolds Farley, 141–210. New York: Russell Sage.

Hirschman, Charles, Philip Kasinitz, and Josh DeWind, eds. 1999. *The Handbook of International Migration: The American Experience.* New York: Russell Sage.

Holloway, Steven, Mark Ellis, Richard Wright, and Margaret Hudson. 2005. "Partnering 'Out' and Fitting In: Residential Segregation and the Neighbourhood Contexts of Mixed-Race Households." *Population and Space* 11: 299–324.

Iceland, John. 2004. "Beyond Black and White: Residential Segregation in Multiethnic America." *Social Science Research* 33, 2 (June): 248–71.

Iceland, John, and Kyle Anne Nelson. 2008. "Hispanic Segregation in Metropolitan America: Exploring the Multiple Forms of Spatial Assimilation." *American Sociological Review* 73, 5:741–65.

Iceland, John, and Melissa Scopilliti. 2008. "Immigrant Residential Segregation in U.S. Metropolitan Areas, 1990–2000." *Demography* 45, 1:79–94.

Iceland, John, Daniel H. Weinberg, and Erika Steinmetz. 2002. *Racial and Eth-*

nic Residential Segregation in the United States: 1980–2000. U.S. Census Bureau, Census Special Report, CENSR-3. Washington, D.C.: U.S. Government Printing Office.

Iceland, John, and Rima Wilkes. 2006. "Does Socioeconomic Status Matter? Race, Class, and Residential Segregation." *Social Problems* 52, 2:248–73.

Itzigsohn, Jose. 2004. "The Formation of Latino and Latina Panethnic Identities." In *Not Just Black and White: Historical and Contemporary Perspectives on Immigration, Race, and Ethnicity in the United States*, edited by Nancy Foner and George M. Frederickson, 197–216. New York: Russell Sage.

Jargowsky, Paul. 1996. *Poverty and Place: Ghettos, Barrios, and the American City.* New York: Russell Sage.

Jeffreys, Kelly. 2007. *U.S. Legal Permanent Residents: 2006.* Department of Homeland Security, Office of Immigration Statistics, Annual Flow Report. Washington, D.C.: U.S. Government Printing Office.

Johnson, James H., Walter C. Farrell Jr., and Chandra Guinn. 1999. "Immigration Reform and the Browning of America: Tension, Conflicts, and Community Instability in Metropolitan Los Angeles." In *The Handbook of International Migration*, edited by Charles Hirschman, Philip Kasinitz, and Josh DeWind, 390–411. New York: Russell Sage.

Johnston, Ron, Michael Poulsen, and James Forrest. 2006. "Blacks and Hispanics in Urban America: Similar Patterns of Residential Segregation?" *Population, Space, and Place* 12:389–406.

Jones, Nicholas A., and Amy Symens Smith. 2001. *The Two or More Races Population: 2000.* U.S. Census Bureau, Census 2000 Brief, C2KBR/01-6. Washington, D.C.: U.S. Government Printing Office.

Kasinitz, Philip. 2004. "Race, Assimilation, and 'Second Generations,' Past and Present." In *Not Just Black and White: Historical and Contemporary Perspectives on Immigration, Race, and Ethnicity in the United States*, edited by Nancy Foner and George M. Frederickson, 278–98. New York: Russell Sage.

Kasinitz, Philip, John H. Mollenkopf, and Mary C. Waters. 2004. "Worlds of the Second Generation." In *Becoming New Yorkers: Ethnographies of the New Second Generation*, edited by Philip Kasinitz, John H. Mollenkopf, and Mary C. Waters, 1–19. New York: Russell Sage.

Kim, Dae Young. 2004. "Leaving the Ethnic Economy: The Rapid Integration of Second-Generation Korean Americans in New York." In *Becoming New Yorkers: Ethnographies of the New Second Generation*, edited by Philip Kasinitz, John H. Mollenkopf, and Mary C. Waters, 154–88. New York: Russell Sage.

Krivo, Lauren J., and Robert L. Kaufman. 1999. "How Low Can It Go? Declining Black-White Segregation in a Multiethnic Context." *Demography* 36, 1:93–109.

Krysan, Maria. 2002. "Whites Who Say They'd Flee: Who Are They, and Why Would They Leave?" *Demography* 39, 4:675–96.

Landale, Nancy S., and R. S. Oropesa. 2002. "White, Black, or Puerto Rican? Racial Self-Identification among Mainland and Island Puerto Ricans." *Social Forces* 81, 1:231–54.

Lee, Jennifer, and Frank D. Bean. 2007. "Redrawing the Line?" *City and Community* 6, 1:49–62.

Lee, Sharon, and Barry Edmonston. 2005. "New Marriages, New Families: U.S. Racial and Hispanic Intermarriage." *Population Bulletin* 60, 2:1–36.

Lewis Mumford Center. 2001a. American Communities Project, Metropolitan Racial and Ethnic Change—Census 2000. www.s4.brown.edu/cen2000/WholePop/WPsegdata.htm (retrieved July 12, 2007).

———. 2001b. *Ethnic Diversity Grows, Neighborhood Integration Lags Behind.* Albany: Lewis Mumford Center, State University of New York, December.

Li, John. 2004. "The Black-Asian Conflict?" In *Not Just Black and White: Historical and Contemporary Perspectives on Immigration, Race, and Ethnicity in the United States,* edited by Nancy Foner and George M. Frederickson, 301–14. New York: Russell Sage.

Lieberson, Stanley. 1980. *A Piece of the Pie: Blacks and White Immigrants since 1980.* Berkeley: University of California Press.

Lindsay, James M., and Audrey Singer. 2003. "Changing Faces: Immigrants and Diversity in the Twenty-first Century." In *Agenda for the Nation,* edited by Henry J. Aaron, James M. Lindsay, and Pietro S. Nivola. Washington, D.C.: Brookings Institution Press.

Logan, John R. 2002a. *Choosing Segregation: Racial Imbalance in American Public Schools, 1990–2000.* Lewis Mumford Center, March 29. www.s4.brown.edu/cen2000/SchoolPop/SPReport/page1.html (retrieved June 15, 2007).

———. 2002b. *Hispanic Populations and Their Residential Patterns in the Metropolis.* Lewis Mumford Center, May 8. http://mumford.albany.edu/census/HispanicPop/HspReportNew/MumfordReport.pdf (retrieved June 21, 2007).

———. 2003. *How Race Counts for Hispanic Americans.* Lewis Mumford Center, July 14. http://mumford.albany.edu/census/report.html (retrieved June 8, 2007).

Logan, John R., Richard D. Alba, and Wenquan Zhang. 2002. "Immigrant

Enclaves and Ethnic Communities in New York and Los Angeles." *American Sociological Review* 67:299–322.

Logan, John R., Brian J. Stults, and Reynolds Farley. 2004. "Segregation of Minorities in the Metropolis: Two Decades of Change." *Demography* 41, 1:1–22.

Logan, John R., and Charles Zhang. 2007. "Global Neighborhoods: Pathways to Diversity and Separation." Paper presented at the annual meetings of the Population Association of America, New York, March 29–31.

Maly, Michael T. 2000. "The Neighborhood Diversity Index." *Journal of Urban Affairs* 22, 1:37–47.

———. 2005. *Beyond Segregation: Multiracial and Multiethnic Neighborhoods in the United States*. Philadelphia: Temple University Press.

Martin, Michael E. 2007. *Residential Segregation Patterns of Latinos in the United States, 1990–2000: Testing the Ethnic Enclave and Inequality Theories*. New York: Routledge.

Martin, Philip, and Elizabeth Midgley. 2003. "Immigration: Shaping and Reshaping America." *Population Bulletin* 58, 2 (June): 1–44.

———. 2006. "Immigration: Shaping and Reshaping America." *Population Bulletin* 61, 4 (December): 1–28.

Massey, Douglas S. 2002. *The River: The Social Origin of Freshmen at America's Selective Colleges and Universities*. Princeton, NJ: Princeton University Press.

———. 2004. "Segregation and Stratification: A Biosocial Perspective." *Du Bois Review* 1, 1:7–25.

———. 2007. *Categorically Unequal: The American Stratification System*. New York: Russell Sage.

Massey, Douglas S., and Nancy A. Denton. 1987. "Trends in the Residential Segregation of Blacks, Hispanics, and Asians." *American Sociological Review* 50:802–25.

———. 1988. "The Dimensions of Residential Segregation." *Social Forces* 67, 2:281–315.

———. 1989. "Hypersegregation in U.S. Metropolitan Areas: Black and Hispanic Segregation along Five Dimensions." *Demography* 26, 3:373–93.

———. 1993. *American Apartheid: Segregation and the Making of the Underclass*. Cambridge: Harvard University Press.

Migration Policy Institute. 2007. "States Ranked by Number of Foreign Born: 1990, 2000, and 2005." MPI Data Hub, 2005 American Community Survey and Census Data on the Foreign Born by State. www.migrationinformation.org/datahub/acscensus.cfm (retrieved May 21, 2007).

Modan, Gabriella Gahlia. 2007. *Turf Wars: Discourse, Diversity, and the Politics of Place*. Malden, MA: Blackwell.

Myrdal, Gunnar. 1944. *An American Dilemma: The Negro Problem and Modern Democracy*. Reprint, New Brunswick, NJ: Transaction, 1996.

National Research Council. 2006. *Multiple Origins, Uncertain Destinies: Hispanics and the American Future*. Edited by Marta Tienda and Faith Mitchell. Washington, D.C.: National Academies Press.

Oropesa, R. S., Nancy S. Landale, and Meredith J. Greif. Forthcoming. "From Puerto Rican to Pan-Ethnic in New York City." *Ethnic and Racial Studies*.

Park, Robert E. 1925. "The City: Suggestions for the Investigation of Human Behavior in the Urban Environment." In *The City*, edited by Robert E. Park and Ernest W. Burgess, 1–46. Chicago: Chicago University Press.

Park, Robert E., and Ernest W. Burgess. 1921. *Introduction to the Science of Sociology*. Reprint, Chicago: University of Chicago Press, 1969.

Park, Robert E., Ernest W. Burgess, and Roderik D. McKenzie. 1925. *The City*. Chicago: Chicago University Press.

Passel, Jeffrey S. 2007. *Unauthorized Migrants: Numbers and Characteristics*. Pew Hispanic Center Research Report, June 14. http://pewhispanic.org/reports/report.php?ReportID=46 (retrieved July 2, 2007).

Perlmann, Joel, and Mary C. Waters. 2004. "Intermarriage Then and Now: Race, Generation, and the Changing Meaning of Marriage." In *Not Just Black and White: Historical and Contemporary Perspectives on Immigration, Race, and Ethnicity in the United States*, edited by Nancy Foner and George M. Frederickson, 262–77. New York: Russell Sage.

Portes, Alejandro, and Ruben G. Rumbaut. 2001. *Legacies: The Story of the Immigrant Second Generation*. Berkeley: University of California Press.

———. 2006. *Immigrant America: A Portrait*. 3rd ed. Berkeley: University of California Press.

Portes, Alejandro, and Min Zhou. 1993. "The New Second Generation: Segmented Assimilation and Its Variants among Post-1965 Immigrant Youth." *Annals of the American Academy of Political and Social Science* 530 (November): 74–96.

Prewitt, Kenneth. "The Census Counts, the Census Classifies." 2004. In *Not Just Black and White: Historical and Contemporary Perspectives on Immigration, Race, and Ethnicity in the United States*, edited by Nancy Foner and George M. Frederickson, 154–64. New York: Russell Sage.

Putnam, Robert D. 2007. "*E Pluribus Unum:* Diversity and Community in the

Twenty-first Century; The 2006 Johan Skytte Prize Lecture." *Scandinavian Political Studies* 30, 2:137–74.

Qian, Zhenchao, and Daniel T. Lichter. 2007. "Social Boundaries and Marital Assimilation: Interpreting Trends in Racial and Ethnic Intermarriage." *American Sociological Review* 72:68–94.

Reardon, Sean F., and Glenn Firebaugh. 2002. "Measures of MultiGroup Segregation." *Sociological Methodology* 32, 1:33–67.

Reardon, Sean F., and David O'Sullivan. 2004. "Measures of Spatial Segregation." *Sociological Methodology* 34, 1:121–62.

Rodriguez, Nestor. 1999. "U.S. Immigration and Changing Relations between African Americans and Latinos." In *The Handbook of International Migration*, edited by Charles Hirschman, Philip Kasinitz, and Josh DeWind, 423–32. New York: Russell Sage.

Ross, Stephen L., and Margery Austin Turner. 2005. "Housing Discrimination in Metropolitan America: Explaining Changes between 1989 and 2000." *Social Problems* 52, 2:152–80.

Rucker, Philip, and Avis Thomas-Lester. 2007. "Shifting Migration Patterns Alter Portrait of Pr. George's." *Washington Post*, July 26, A01.

Rumbaut, Ruben G. 2006. "The Making of a People" In *Hispanics and the Future of America*, edited by Marta Tienda and Faith Mitchell, 16–65. Washington, D.C.: National Academies Press.

Sakamoto, Arthur, Huei-Hsia Wu, and Jessie M. Tzeng. 2000. "The Declining Significance of Race among American Men during the Latter Half of the Twentieth Century." *Demography* 37, 1:41–51.

Sandefur, Gary D., Molly Martin, Jennifer Eggerling-Boeck, Susan E. Mannon, and Ann M. Meier. 2001. "An Overview of Racial and Ethnic Demographic Trends." In *America Becoming: Racial Trends and Their Consequences*, vol. 1, edited by Neil J. Smelser, William Julius Wilson, and Faith Mitchell, 40–102. Washington, D.C.: National Academies Press.

Sandoval, Juan Oneisimo, Hans P. Johnson, and Sonya M. Tafoya. 2002. "Who's Your Neighbor? Residential Segregation in California." *California Counts: Population Trends and Profiles* (Public Policy Institute of California) 4, 1 (August): 1–19.

Santiago, Anna M., and Margaret G. Wilder. 1991. "Residential Segregation and Links to Minority Poverty: The Case for Latino in the United States," *Social Problems* 38, 4 (November): 492–515.

Scopilliti, Melissa, and John Iceland. 2008. "Residential Patterns of Black Immigrants and Native-Born Blacks in the United States." *Social Science Quarterly* 89, 3:547–72.

Singer, Audrey. 2003. *At Home in the Nation's Capital: Immigrant Trends in Metropolitan Washington.* Washington, D.C.: Brookings Institution Center on Urban and Metropolitan Policy, Greater Washington Research Program, June.

———. 2004. *The Rise of New Immigrant Gateways.* Living Cities Census Series. Washington, D.C.: Brookings Institution Center on Urban and Metropolitan Policy, February.

Singer, Audrey, Samantha Friedman, Ivan Cheung, and Marie Price. 2001. *The World in a Zip Code: Greater Washington, D.C. as a New Region of Immigration.* Washington, D.C.: Brookings Institution Center on Urban and Metropolitan Policy, Greater Washington Research Program, April.

South, Scott J., Kyle Crowder, and Erick Chavez. 2005a. "Geographic Mobility and Spatial Assimilation among U.S. Latino Immigrants." *International Migration Review* 39, 3:577–607.

———. 2005b. "Migration and Spatial Assimilation among U.S. Latinos: Classic versus Segmented Trajectories." *Demography* 42, 3:497–521.

Squires, Gregory D., and Charis E. Kurbin. 2006. *Privileged Places: Race, Residence, and the Structure of Opportunity.* Boulder, CO: Lynne Rienner.

Taeuber, Karl E., and Alma F. Taeuber. 1965. Negroes in Cities: Residential Segregation and Neighborhood Change. Chicago: Aldine.

Tejos, Nancy. 2007. "Testing the Boundaries: Latinos Trade Renting in Familiar Enclaves for Owning East of the Anacostia." *Washington Post*, June 9, F01.

Theil, Henry. 1972. *Statistical Decomposition Theory.* New York: American Elsevier.

Timberlake, Jeffrey, and John Iceland. 2007. "Change in Racial and Ethnic Residential Inequality in American Cities, 1970–2000." *City and Community* 6, 4:335–65.

Tocqueville, Alexis de. 1835. *Democracy in America.* Reprint, New York: Penguin Putnam, 2004.

Turner, Margery Austin, and Stephen L. Ross. 2003. *Discrimination in Metropolitan Housing Markets: Phase 2—Asians and Pacific Islanders of the HDS 2000.* Washington, D.C.: U.S. Department of Housing and Urban Development.

———. 2005. "Racial Discrimination and the Housing Search." In *The Geography of Opportunity*, edited by Xavier de Souza Briggs. Washington, D.C.: Brookings Institution Press.

Turner, Margery Austin, Stephen L. Ross, George Galster, and John Yinger. 2002. *Discrimination in Metropolitan Housing Markets: National Results from Phase 1 of the Housing Discrimination Study (HDS)*. Washington, D.C.: U.S. Department of Housing and Urban Development.

U.S. Census Bureau. 2000a. "DP-2 Profile of Selected Social Characteristics: 2000." Census 2000 Summary File 3 (SF 3) Sample Data, Census Tract 114, Kings County, New York. Available at U.S. Census Bureau, American Fact-Finder, http://factfinder.census.gov (retrieved July 6, 2007).

———. 2000b. "DP-2 Profile of Selected Social Characteristics: 2000," Census 2000 Summary File 3 (SF 3) Sample Data, Silver Spring, Maryland. Available at U.S. Census Bureau, American FactFinder, http://factfinder.census.gov (retrieved April 1, 2007).

———. 2000c. "QT-P4. Race, Combinations of Two Races, and Not Hispanic or Latino: 2000." Census 2000 Summary File 1 100-Percent Data. Available at U.S. Census Bureau, American FactFinder, http://factfinder.census.gov (retrieved April 1, 2007).

———. 2001. "Hispanic or Latino by Specific Origin." Census 2000 Summary File 1 100-Percent Data, Table PCT11. Available at U.S. Census Bureau, American FactFinder, http://factfinder.census.gov (retrieved April 1, 2007).

———. 2003. "Table NST-EST2003-04—Cumulative Estimates of the Components of Population Change for the United States and States: April 1, 2000 to July 1, 2003." U.S. Census Bureau, Population Division, December 18. www.census.gov/popest/states/tables/NST-EST2003-04.pdf (retrieved April 3, 2007).

———. 2005a. *Peer Review of "Racial and Ethnic Residential Segregation in the United States: 1980–2000."* U.S. Census Bureau, January. www.census.gov/hhes/www/housing/resseg/peer_review.html (retrieved July 3, 2007).

———. 2005b. "Place of Birth for the Foreign-Born Population." American Community Survey data, Table B05006. Available at U.S. Census Bureau, American FactFinder, http://factfinder.census.gov (retrieved May 30, 2007).

———. 2006a. "Fairfax County, Virginia Data Profile: 2005." American Community Survey data. Available at U.S. Census Bureau, American FactFinder, http://factfinder.census.gov (retrieved June 28, 2007).

———. 2006b. "Median Household Income in the Past 12 Months (in 2005 Inflation-Adjusted Dollars)." American Community Survey 2005 data, Tables B19013B, B19013D, B19013H, B19013I. Available at U.S. Census

Bureau, American FactFinder, http://factfinder.census.gov (retrieved May 30, 2007).

———. 2006c. "Race." American Community Survey 2005 data, Table B02001. Available at U.S. Census Bureau, American FactFinder, http://factfinder .census.gov (retrieved June 18, 2007).

———. 2006d. "United States Population and Housing Narrative Profile: 2005." American Community Survey data. Available at U.S. Census Bureau, American FactFinder, http://factfinder.census.gov (retrieved May 30, 2007).

———. 2006e. "Washington-Arlington-Alexandria, DC-VA-MD-WV Metropolitan Statistical Area Population and Housing Narrative Profile: 2005." American Community Survey data. Available at U.S. Census Bureau, American FactFinder, http://factfinder.census.gov (retrieved May 30, 2007).

U.S. Immigration and Naturalization Service. 2002. *Statistical Yearbook of the Immigration and Naturalization Service, 2000*. Washington, D.C.: U.S. Government Printing Office.

Van Dyne, Larry. 2006. "A Million Strong." *Washingtonian* (October 6): 86–89.

Waters, Mary C. 1990. *Ethnic Options: Choosing Identities in America*. Berkeley: University of California Press.

———. 1994. "Ethnic and Racial Identities of Second-Generation Black Immigrants in New York City." *International Migration Review* 28, 4:795–820.

Western, Bruce. 2006. *Punishment and Inequality in America*. New York: Russell Sage.

White, Michael J. 1983. "The Measurement of Spatial Segregation." *American Journal of Sociology* 88, 5:1008–18.

———. 1987. *American Neighborhoods and Residential Differentiation*. New York: Russell Sage.

White, Michael J., and Jennifer E. Glick. 1999. "The Impact of Immigration on Residential Segregation." In *Immigration and Opportunity*, edited by Frank D. Bean and Stephanie Bell-Rose, 345–72. New York: Russell Sage.

White, Michael J., Ann H. Kim, and Jennifer E. Glick. 2005. "Mapping Social Distance: Ethnic Residential Segregation in a Multiethnic Metro." *Sociological Methods and Research* 34, 2:173–203.

White, Michael J., and Sharon Sassler. 2000. "Judging Not Only by Color: Ethnicity, Nativity, and Neighborhood Attainment." *Social Science Quarterly* 81, 4:997–1013.

Wilson, William Julius, and Richard P. Taub. 2006. *There Goes the Neighborhood*. New York: Alfred A. Knopf.

Wingett, Yvonne. 2007. "Mexican Immigrants Find Community in Phoenix Neighborhoods." Associated Press, March 25.

Wirth, Louis. 1928. *The Ghetto.* Chicago: University of Chicago Press.

Wong, David S. 1993. "Spatial Indices of Segregation." *Urban Studies* 30, 3:559–72.

Yinger, John. 1995. *Closed Doors, Opportunities Lost: The Continuing Costs of Housing Discrimination.* New York: Russell Sage.

Zangwill, Israel. 2006. *From the Ghetto to the Melting Pot: Israel Zangwill's Jewish Plays; Three Playscripts.* Detroit: Wayne State University Press.

Zhou, Min. 1999. "Segmented Assimilation: Issues, Controversies, and Recent Research on the New Second Generation." In *The Handbook of International Migration: The American Experience,* edited by Charles Hirschman, Philip Kasinitz, and Josh DeWind, 172–95. New York: Russell Sage.

INDEX

acculturation, 7–8, 68–78, 96–102, 193n19; and ethnic disadvantage, 29; residential segregation and, 23–24, 69, 77–78, 138; vs. structural assimilation, 18. *See also* education; English-language ability

African Americans, 144; black immigrant segregation from, 90, 103, 105; declining segregation, 41–50, 104, 110–15, 138; diversity levels affecting segregation of, 110–15, **112**, 131; ghettos, 44, 45, 129; Hispanic segregation from, 5, 85–91, **87**, 98–105, **99**, 133, 153; information theory index, 110; isolation index, 42–**43**; migration to cities, 44; reference group in segregation calculations, 86–87, **92–95**, 98; regional settlement, 38; SES, 9, 46–52, **47**, 60–61; slavery, 16, 79, 81; suburbanization, 38; U.S. population (2005), 31; Washington, D.C., 60–61, 63, 89, 120–21, 122–23. *See also* black-white divide

African immigrants, 178n14; percent of immigrants (1900–1920 and 1980–2000), **36**–37; regional settlement of refugees, 38; Washington, D.C., 39, 61, 63, 120. *See also* black immigrants; Caribbeans; Nigerians

agricultural jobs, 34–35

Alaska Natives: census category, 143, 149; segregation changes (1980–2000), 110

Alba, Richard, 24, 26, 84–85, 122

alienation, immigrant, 10

Alinsky, Saul, 115–16

Amendments to Immigration and Nationality Act (Hart-Celler Act, 1965 reforms), 31–32, 35, 80

American Apartheid (Massey and Denton), 6, 9, 21–22, 51, 52

American Dilemma: The Negro Problem and Modern Democracy (Myrdal), 19

American Indians: census category, 143, 149; difficulty studying, 144; segregation changes (1980–2000), 110; U.S. population (2005), 31; Washington, D.C., 60; white immigrant warfare with, 14, 79

Text: 10/15 Janson
Display: Janson
Compositor: BookMatters, Berkeley
Indexer: Barbara Roos
Printer and binder: Maple-Vail Book Manufacturing Group